Treasured Qigong of Traditional Medical School

Huang Runtian

© Hai Feng Publishing Co.

TREASURED QIGONG OF
TRADITIONAL MEDICAL SCHOOL

Written by
Huang Runtian

Translated by
Chen Guansheng

Art edited by
Ki-Coo Seto

Published by
Hai Feng Publishing Co.
Rm. 1502, Wing On House,
71 Des Voeux Road, C.,
Hong Kong

Printed by
Friendly Printing Co., Ltd.
Flat B1, 3/F., Luen Ming Hing Ind. Bldg.,
36 Muk Cheong St., Tokwawan, Kowloon

First Edition February 1994

ISBN 962-238-209-6
HF-231-P

CONTENTS

ABOUT THE AUTHOR

Mr. Huang Runtian comes of a traditional-Chinese-medicine family. This provided him with ample opportunity to study traditional Chinese medicine and the Treasured Qigong Exercises of the Medical School in the days of his youth. Thanks to his ability, he has obtained great success, and he has become the only Master of the Treasured Qigong of the Medical School.

Mr. Huang Runtian took over his father's career and developed it. During the recent years he devoted himself to spreading the Treasured Qigong Exercise of the Medical School, which had been kept a secret by the older generations. He toured around the country and went abroad to give lectures on the theory and method of the Treasured Qigong, gave treatment to patients, cured numerous patients, and trained hundreds of clinical professionals of the Treasured Qigong. His deeds and Qigong maneuvers have been publicized by media at home and abroad. He is a distinguished senior Qigong master.

Mr. Huang is now the Vice President of the China Folk Qigong Science Research Society, in charge of the Qigong exchange with Japan and Southeast Asia. He is also director, special member, and senior advisor of many Qigong research organizations at home and abroad.

Mr. Huang now works with the Qigong Immunization Clinic of the Naval General Hospital, engaging in Qigong medicine, teaching and research work, and he has achieved excellent results.

◆

PREFACE

The methods of Traditional Chinese Qigong exercises vary among different sects and schools—the Confucian School, the Buddhist School, the Taoist School, the Medical School, and the *Wushu* (Chinese martial arts) School. In addition, there are many other folk Qigong exercises practiced among the people at home and abroad. Qigong of the Chinese Medical School, or the Medical Qigong, has a distinctive style. For thousands of years Qigong of the Chinese Medical School has played a great role in resisting premature aging, promoting health, preventing diseases and prolonging life. It has also made great contributions to the prosperity of the cause of Qigong and civilization.

The *Internal Canon of Medicine* (*Huangdi Neijing*), a Chinese medical classic book written more than two thousand years ago, laid the theoretical foundation of Qigong and made a concrete record of Qigong exercises. It emphasizes that for the Medical School the main purpose of doing Qigong exercises is to treat diseases, strengthen the constitution, resist premature aging and prolong life.

The *Internal Canon of Medicine* (*Huangdi Neijing*) states: "Remain nonchalant and void, then genuine Qi will follow; keep a sound mind, how can diseases come on." The statement is still significant to the people doing Qigong exercises up to the present. A great many of eminent doctors of traditional Chinese medicine of past generations studied Qigong and achieved success. For instance, the founder of the Traditional Chinese Medicine Pian Gu stated: "If you drink the water of *Shangchi*, you will gain an insight into *Yuan Yi Fang Ren*." Doctor Hua Tuo (2nd century), a master of surgery, invented Qigong exercises imitating the movements of five animals, called "The Frolics of Five Animals." Doctor Zhang Zhongjing, a great master of medicine, invented the methods of expiration, inhalation and induction of Qi, "*Dao-yin, Tu-na*." In the Ming Dynasty, the renowned pharmacologist Li Shizheng (1518-1593) stated: "The inner scene and channels can be perceived clearly only by those who can see inwards." From these statements it can be seen that the Qigong of Medical School has a long history and is deep-rooted.

The classics of Traditional Chinese Medicine all have a concise exposition of the theory and methods of Qigong exercises. Besides, there are also many good methods of the Qigong exercises passed orally from generation to generation. Qigong exercises of the Medical School are in accordance with an objective law: "A wide road is simple." Though the theory on Qigong exercises is fragmentary in the classics, the *Internal Canon of Medicine* says: "What is inside shows itself outside." It means the Qigong of Medical School is just like a "divine dragon with a visible head and an invisible tail." However, the Qigong of Medical School as a complete system with rich content is really worthy of careful study.

Theoretically, the Qigong is based on such theories of the Traditional Chinese Medicine as *Yi-Li* (the Way of Change), *Yin-Yang*, *Wuxing* (the Five Elements), *Bagua* (the Eight Diagrams), relation between heaven and human beings, the concept of viewing the body as a whole, and doctrines on internal organs of the body and channels and collaterals. Chinese physicians of past generations practiced various Qigong exercises of the Traditional Medical School for the purpose of promoting health and prolonging life as well as curing diseases with Qi. Zhang Xichun, a well-known doctor of modern times, maintains that physicians should do Qigong exercises. He holds that for physicians to do Qigong can promote their health and raise their professional medical level: it can "strengthen their bones and improve their intelligence," and it can make them "see their viscera as clearly as a lightning" and thus result in "understanding the truth of life and the way of protecting health." The statement was penetrating, because it summarized the benefits of the Qigong of Medical School.

I learned medicine first from my father and then from other tutors. Since I became a physician I have realized through clinical practice that the Qigong of Medical School is a complete scientific system of practical Qigong, and that it has the ability to save a patient from critical condition. Many patients recovered their health with Qigong treatment. The main effects of Qigong are as follows: curing diseases, promoting health, improving intelligence and figure building, protecting vitality, and prolonging life. The Qigong exercises are simple and have immediate efficacy. Every one can be benefited from Qigong. The way of learning Qigong is flexible. One can learn step by step the whole system of Qigong or a part of it, and it is convenient and easy to learn. It is just like what the saying goes: "a wide road is simple."

Qigong exercises of the Medical School are harmonious with those of other schools, each benefiting from association with the other. As proved by facts, any one who adopts the Medical Qigong after practicing some other regular Qigong patterns can achieve better results from Qigong exercises, increasing his intelligence and activate his body energy. The Medical Qigong has all along persisted in taking in strong points of other schools, learning from them and being able to exist together with them.

The theory of the Medical Qigong is based on traditional Chinese medical theory, emphasizing the regulation of internal organs and maintaining a balance between Yin and Yang, Qi and blood. The Qigong of the Medical School considers restoring prenatal and postnatal vital energy as its chief aim. After learning the Qigong for a short time, one, whether a man or a woman, old or young, can master it. Persisting in practicing the Qigong, one will be healthy physically and mentally and will enjoy a prolonging life. A systematic training will lead to great effects such as *pi-gu* (fast), activate body energy, and give medical treatment at a distance. In a word, the practice of the Qigong has the function of medical treatment, promotion of health and prolongation of life.

The Central People's Broadcasting Station made a series of introduction of the Treasured Qigong of the Medical School and showed how I practiced and spread it through a program named "Friendship Through Broadcast" during the Christmas holidays of 1989. The introduction was entitled "The Medical Qigong is of long standing. The Medical Qigong benefits the people." Then China Broadcast and TV Press published my *Qigong Therapy* in March 1991, which is a part of my experiences in spreading the Qigong of theMedical School. Tianjin Audio-Video Company published my tape cassette about the Qigong of Medical School (made under the supervision of China Association of Popular Qigong). Now, in order to meet the demand of various circles, I systematized the main methods of the Medical Qigong and my teaching experience of many years into this book with the aim of spreading the Qigong of Medical School at home and abroad and bring benefits to mankind.

Huang Runtian, March 1991,
in Beijing

PART ONE

THE TREASURED QIGONG EXERCISES OF MEDICAL SCHOOL

The Qigong of Medical School, or the Medical Qigong, lays stress on practice and efficacy. Its practice is simple and its theory is stated precisely. It has the functions of preventing and curing diseases, strengthening health, improving intelligence and prolonging life.

The Medical Qogong involves a series of exercises, which you can practice wholly or selectively according to your own needs. It can also be practiced together with Qigong exercises of other schools, but they must not be practiced at the same time. Only in this way may the practitioner gain benefits from them.

I practiced it myself and got benefits from it. Then I spread it among the people. Whoever practices it has his health strengthened greatly.

The Medical Qigong aims at, first of all, getting rid of diseases. Having laid a sound foundation to it, the practitioner can enhance the Qigong effects and exploit potential energy. At the beginning a practitioner will find the Qigong can make him feel bright-eyed and clear-headed. After doing it for a period of time he will find his health in excellent condition. The Qigong exercise of "An Internal View of the Five Parenchymatous Viscera" is really a hope to patients, a ladder leading to sound health, a talisman for enhancing the Qigong efficacy. The "Qigong of Invigorating Kidney and Adjusting Qi" is a really miraculous cure which can invigorate the function of the kidney and brain, strengthen bones and promote the marrow. The "Basic Qigong Exercise for Universal Illumination and Emitting-Qi" can strengthen health and cure diseases. The "Qigong Massage Recipes" are simple as well as practical. The "Bathing and Purifying Body Qigong" can develop intelligence and improve ability, and it is fascinating. If you keep on practicing it, you will gain boundless magic efficacy. The "Purplish Rays of Light Penetrating Body Qigong" can link practitioners with the nature permanently, and they can enjoy beautiful "scenery" heartily. The "Unification of Mind-will and Qi Exercise" is a very good ABC exercise for advanced maneuvers, which will improve the practitioner's intelligence.

One of the reasons why it is called the Qigong of the Medical School, or the Medical Qigong, is that its theory is based on the Traditional Chinese Medicine. They are actually an integral whole, but the Qigong is more fascinating with its "magic power" than the Traditional Chinese Medicine. Another reason is that it is especially appropriate for the Traditional Chinese Medicine workers and enthusiasts to practice. We would like to offer the Qigong to the Chinese people and to my friends. We hope they all will enjoy the fascinating world created by the Treasured Qigong of the Medical School.

Five Fundamental Postures of the Medical School Qigong Exercises

Fig. 1
Double Cross-legged sitting posture.

Fig. 2
Single Cross-legged sitting posture.

Fig. 3
Natural cross-legged sitting posture.

Fig. 4
Simple sitting posture.

Fig. 5
Standing posture.

I. Fundamental Qigong Exercises
Five Qigong Exercises of the Medical School

1. The Qigong of Invigorating the Kidney and Adjusting the Qi (*Tong-yuan-ji-ji-gong*).

The Qigong of Invigorating the Kidney and Adjusting Qi (vital energy), an important branch of Chinese traditional Medical School Qigong, has a long history. Having been tested in practice and by time, the Qigong exercise proves itself to have the functions of curing diseases, strengthening health, improving intelligence, exploiting potential energy and prolonging life. The Qigong exercise is easy to learn and its theory is profound but its methods are simple. The Qigong will not cause mental disorder. Instead the practitioner will get immediate good results from it. Thus every one can practice it.

In practicing the Qigong, the practitioner need not believe in it, but he must do the exercises earnestly. The practitioner will get benefits from it, whether he believes it or not. It is easy to master. Those who keep on practicing it will no doubt be healthy physically and mentally and will enjoy a long life.

(1) Exercises.

Take a sitting posture (cross-legged or simple-sitting to your need). Close eyes slightly. Rid the mind of all distractions. Relax the whole body. Breath naturally. Keep this situation for a quarter of an hour.

Then open the eyes. Put the right foot on the left knee (a reverse for females). Tap the arch of the right foot with the palm of the left hand, with the Laogong acupoint tapping the Yongquan acupoint (see No.8 on the Diagram of Acupoints). While tapping, concentrate your mind and have the idea "tap hard," but tap with an even and proper force, not with a stiff hand (Fig.6). After that do the same thing to the other foot (Figs. 7 and 8).

(2) Frequency and duration of exercise.

For health protection, once a day before going to bed in the evening; for clinical treatment, three to five times a day.

The times of beating: 100 for each foot on the first day; 200 the second day; 300 from the third day on. The times can be increased according to your need, but should not be over 900.

(3) Points for attention.

a. Do not beat hard. To keep the idea "Beat it hard," but do it with an even force is a principle.

b. It is normal that a beginner would feel a little hot and pain and have a swelling at the soles and palms. But the heat, pain and swelling will be released if he weakens the strength of beating (but he must not give up the idea "Beat it hard"). When the channels of Qi and acupoint lines are dredged, the bad reaction will disappear.

c. When you practice the Qigong exercise of the Medical School, you must not mix it with any other Qigong exercises (not even a part of them). You can do other Qigong exercises when you do not do the Qigong exercise of the Medical School, i.e., it can be done together with other ones but at different time.

d. To end the exercise, calm down again for a quarter of an hour. The ending form is the same as the starting form.

e. Having done the exercise, the practitioner, if he suffers from low blood-pressure and insufficient blood sugar, he or she must put his left or her right palm on the head with Laogong acupoint (No.8 on the Diagram of Acupoints) facing Baihui acupoint (No. 12)

Fig. 6

The Qigong of invigorating the Kidney and Adjusting the Qi
(*Tong-yuan-ji-ji-gong*) (1)

Fig. 7

The Qigong of invigorating the Kidney and Adjusting the Qi
(*Tong-yuan-ji-ji-gong*) (2)

Fig. 8

The Qigong of invigorating the Kidney and Adjusting the Qi
(*Tong-yuan-ji-ji-gong*) (3)

(4) Application and function.

a. The exercise can cure chronic and intractable diseases caused by Yin deficiency and Yang excess, upper excess and lower deficiency, disharmony between heart and kidney and the excessive rise of liver-yang.

b. It can cure various diseases caused by premature aging such as neurosis, neurasthenia, and impairment of the viscera and deficiency of the primordial Qi, heaviness of the head, pain in waist and knees, Qi and blood deficiency, upper heat and lower cold, burning red face, seminal emission and night sweat, dysphoria and palpitation, poor memory and insomnia and mental depression.

c. It can strengthen the kidney: preventing chronic diseases of aging such as pains in the waist, legs and feet; strengthening the kidney and heart: curing the heart and brain blood-vessel diseases.

d. It can nourish the liver and improve eyesight: curing chronic diseases of the liver and gall and eyesight diseases (near-sighted, far-sighted, and poor-sighted).

e. It can increase intelligence and activate body energy: promoting children's physical and mental health, developing their intelligence and exploiting their potential energy.

f. It has the functions of dispersing the stagnant liver-qi. By means of the Qigong people who suffer from excess of seven emotions (namely, joy, anger, anxiety, worry, grief, apprehension, and fright) can release themselves from mental depression and sentimental diseases.

g. The Qigong exercise can set the mind at ease. If you do the Qigong exercise when you feel tired and nervous, you will recover the clearness of the head, calmness of the mind, quick intelligence and vigor. It can treat insomnia.

h. The Qigong exercise can reinforce body resistance to eliminate pathogens: using the Qigong to remedy Qi and blood disorder, rectify the deviation caused by improper practicing of other Qigong exercises, promoting physical resistance against the diseases caused by six pathogenic factors, namely, wind, cold, summer-heat, dampness, dryness, and fire.

i. It can strengthen health and prolong life. The

Qigong is an important means for making communication between the Qi inside and the Qi outside the body and exploit energy of the body. Persisting in practicing it would have the good results of preserving and strengthening health and prolonging life.

(5) Taboo.

The Qigong exercise is a taboo to the following people:

a. people who suffer from serious diseases;

b. psychotic patients;

c. patients with skin diseases such as fungal infection of the hand and foot ringworm, ulcer and swelling.

(6) Theory.

According to Traditional Chinese Medicine theories, kidney is the essence of health. A health body is maintained by sufficient kidney-Qi. The arch at the bottom of the foot is the beginning of kidney channel, and thus is considered as the "root" of "essence." Yongquan acupoint at the arch of the foot is an important point (Jing point) on the kidney channel, which is a key point for the communication between man and earth-Qi. If the acupoint does not work, the kidney-Qi will not go. This would result in water not flowing upward, fire burning without control, and Yin deficiency and Yang excess, which would cause premature aging, insufficiency of the kidney, and weakness in the legs.

The Qigong exercise is dedicated for curing such symptoms as Yin deficiency and Yang excess, and water deficiency and fire excess. Whether they are symptoms of diseases or are caused by wrong practicing of Qigong, they can be treated by means of this Qigong exercise.

The key of this Qigong exercise is Laogong tapping Yongquan and the idea of "beating hard." Through the coordination and communication of acupoints and of channels and collaterals, it results in the harmony between the heart and kidney and the harmony between water and fire. Through tapping, Laogong acupoint continuously gives the external Qi into Yongquan acupoint (but the practitioner should not have the idea in his mind, because the Qi should go into the acupoint in a natural way). This would open the Yongquan acupoint. Once the point is opened, a great amount of the underground energy such as terrestrial magnetism, underground radiation, earth heat (traditionally called earth-Qi) would go through the Yongquan point and transform itself into energy needed by human body. It is no doubt significant for the Qigong masters who emits external Qi (*waiqi*) to treat diseases.

As a result of conscientious practicing of the Qigong exercise, the liver-wood nourished by sufficient kidney-water and abundant "earth Qi" would be full of vigor and vitality. Thus the Qigong can nourish the liver and make eyes clear.

As to the number of beating, it would be 100 on the first day, 200 on the second day and 300 on the third day. 300 is the maximum number. The number is accepted according to *Book of Laozi*, which says: "From *Tao* (the Way) grows number one; from number one grows number two, from number two grows number three; from number three grow all things in the world." The word "grow" is the base of the number three.

As proved by a great deal of practice, this Qigong exercise has good efficacy. Its characteristics can be summarized as the following: the exercise is simple and brings about a prompt result; its theory is pregnant with meaning; the simple exercise gives significant results; its practice will bring about wonderful results.

In a word, this Qigong exercise is simple but produces a prompt result. It can treat diseases, correct the deviation occurring in practicing other Qigong exercises, as well as strengthen health and lay a good foundation for further Qigong practicing.

2. The Qigong of an Internal View of the Five Parenchymatous Viscera (*Wu-zang-nei-jing-gong*)

The Qigong of An Internal View of the Five Parenchymatous Viscera is a branch of the Qigong of the Medical School. It was passed down through oral instruction from generation to generation. Having been practiced for a long time, the Qigong exercise is proved to have good effects. It was first introduced to several hundred Qigong followers coming from 27 provinces, cities and autonomous regions at "A Course of Lectures on Clinical Use of Qigong" held by the Jiuxian Qigong Training Center affiliated to the Beijing Association of Qigong in March through April, 1988. After the introduction many people practiced it, and its good efficacy were once more proved.

(1) Postures.

Take a sitting posture (cross-legged or simple). Relax. Put hands and feet in proper position to your convenience. Face the south. Close the eyes slightly.

If taking a standing posture, the practitioner should also face the south. Taking a lying posture, the practitioner may face any direction, but he had better lie on his back. Other requirements are the same as with sitting posture.

(2) Exercise.

Close the eyes slightly. Relax the body for several minutes. Let the mind meet with the divine light, which shine after closing the eyes, and concentrate the mind-will on the kidneys, which are on both sides of the waist. (Need not know their anatomical form and exact position. The same attitude should be applied to the insight viewing on other organs of the body).

Imagine that the kidneys are full of black water. Keep the imagination for several minutes until the imagined object becomes clear in your mind (As to how clear it becomes, it depends on the practitioner's skill and energy, but the practitioner should not strive for it). Then imagine that the black water in the kidneys goes into the Mingmen (gate of life) acupoint at the back waist (see No. 14 on the Diagram of Acupoints) and from the gate of life into the liver. Imagine that the black water goes into the liver and the liver is wholly immersed in the water. Imagine that the water colour changes from black to green. Keep this imagination for several minutes.

Then imagine that the green water goes into the heart in the left thoracic cavity (the practitioner whose heart is in the right thoracic cavity should imagine the water going into the heart at the right). In your imagination the green water in the heart changes into red gas and then from red gas into red light, which pervades, fills and illuminates the whole body. Keep the imagination for several minutes.

Then imagine the red light goes back into the heart and from the heart to Zhongwan acupoint (No. 6), where it changes into a golden round radiance as large as the palm of the hand. Keep the imagination for several minutes.

Then imagine that the golden radiance goes up into the lungs, where it changes into white gas (or white fog or steam). Keep the imagination for several minutes. Then imagine the white gas in the lungs changing into dew drops as clear as those on lotus leaves. The dew drops gather at the Shanzhong acupoint (No. 3) and then from there to Mingmen. From Mingmen the dew drops go by two routes into the kidneys, where they become black water.

(3) Ending exercise.

Open the eyes slowly. Relax and take a standing posture. Tap the whole body with both hands slightly, from head to feet, ten times (Figs. 9-14). This completes the exercise.

Fig. 9

The Qigong of an Internal View of the Five Parenchymatous Viscera (Wu-zang-nei-jing-gong) (1)

Fig. 10

The Qigong of an Internal View of the Five Parenchymatous Viscera (Wu-zang-nei-jing-gong) (2)

Fig. 11

The Qigong of an Internal
View of the Five
Parenchymatous Viscera
(Wu-zang-nei-jing-gong) (3)

Fig. 12

The Qigong of an Internal
View of the Five
Parenchymatous Viscera
(Wu-zang-nei-jing-gong) (4)

Fig. 13

The Qigong of an Internal
View of the Five
Parenchymatous Viscera
(Wu-zang-nei-jing-gong) (5)

Fig. 14

(4) Frequency and duration of the Qigong exercise.

a. For treating diseases, six times a day.

b. For strengthening health and regulating the functions of viscera, three times a day.

c. For doing the Qigong temporarily to accumulate Qi, imagine the five organs of the body each for a few seconds, one after another in sequence as stipulated, but the order of them should not be reversed.

Besides, for doing the Qigong temporarily, need not do the tapping at the end of the exercise; disregard how many times you do it a day but the more the better; each time, three to five minutes will do; there is no strict requirement on the posture and facing direction.

(5) Application.

Those who are in a clear state of mind but suffer from chronic diseases are suitable for this Qigong exercise.

(6) Points for attention.

a. Do not mix this Qigong exercise with other Qigong exercises. When you do this Qigong, you can also do other Qigong exercises, but do not do them at the same time.

b. This Qigong exercise has no taboo and it won't cause side-effects. If you feel bad after doing the Qigong, it is a signal of the disease being under treatment. You should do the Qigong more earnestly so that the disease may be cured.

c. You may do the Qigong when you feel hungry and tired. In that case it will be good for your physical and mental health.

d. A patient suffering from a cold, enteritis, tuberculosis, hepatitis or other acute or chronic disease may do the Qigong to strengthen the resistance against disease and enhance the medical treatment, so that he may recover from the disease as soon as possible.

(7) Theory

The Qigong of an Internal View of the Five Parenchymatous Viscera (*Wu-zang-nei-jing-gong*) is that one takes a view of internal scene of his viscera with his imagination. He does the Qigong exercise to strengthen the functions of his viscera, dredge the channels, keep the balance between Yin and Yang, regulate the coordination between Qi and blood, fill up the deficiency and shun the excess, and exploit potential energy.

The Qigong is based on the theory of the five elements: from water (kidney) comes wood (liver), from wood comes fire (heart), from fire comes earth (spleen and stomach), from earth comes metal (lung) and from metal comes water. The movement of the five elements can exploit the vital energy and vitality inherent in the body and strengthen the functions of channels and collaterals, the viscera, skin, muscles, bones and marrow. Having the effect of "supporting the upright and getting rid of evil," this Qigong exercise can cure various chronic diseases.

This Qigong exercise regards the viscera as a whole, but does not neglect their individuality. Thus it is necessary to direct the intensified Qigong training (prolonging the time of exercise) at the "weak point" of the viscera according to physical condition. So the Qigong can cure diseases, strengthen health, prolong life and promote the effects of Qigong training.

This Qigong exercise pays attention to the essence of vitality (the prenatal essence is in the kidney, and the postnatal essence in the spleen and stomach) and, having found out the basic cause (the viscera being out of coordination) of the ailment, it cures the disease by way of self-regulation according to the Traditional Chinese Medicine theory: "In a deficiency, strengthen the parental viscus, and in an excess, purge the offspring." To regulate the basic cause of ailment is an important Traditional Chinese Medicine principle, which this Qigong exercise observes and which is one of the characteristics of this Qigong.

Experience has proved that some practitioners can visualize their own viscera or those of other people at a distance. It means that they have gained great achievements in the Qigong training. If they keep on training, they will become great Qigong masters.

II. The Qigong for Building the Base

Traditional Qigong theory holds that an adult's body tends to "leak." So it is necessary for him to do Qigong to "repair the leaking body." It means there is something wrong in the body for lack of regulation. According to the Traditional Chinese Medicine theory this indicates the asthenic diseases caused by impairment of the viscera and deficiency of the primordial Qi. The *Internal Canon of Medicine* has a description of it: "A middle aged man is as weak as an old man."

Traditional Chinese Medicine holds that the deficiency syndrome should be treated with tonification (filling up) and support of the primordial Qi. How to tonify (to fill up) the deficiency? "To tonify with food is better than with medicine, but to tonify with Qi is better than with food." How to tonify with Qi? The *Internal Canon of Medicine* says: "The deficiency should be warmed with Qi." It means to nourish Qi by using drugs with warm property. But, if a man suffers asthenic diseases owing to the deficiency of vital essence (*Jing*), Qi and spirit (*Sheng*) and medicine does not work, it is also difficult to recover health only by doing common Qigong exercises.

However, Qigong masters of past generations had invented the secret "Qigong for Building the Base," which is beneficial for tonifying the leaking body. Fortunately, I learned the Qigong. Here I would like to offer it to Qigong lovers. The "Qigong for Building the Base" consists of the following three separate exercises:

a. Gathering Sun Essence Exercise replenishing the Yang-Qi;

b. Gathering Moon Cream Exercise nourishing the Yin-Qi;

c. Postnatal Development Exercise gathering the pure to replace the turbid to strengthen the spleen and stomach and indirectly tonify the prenatal kidney.

All the three Qigong exercises aim to replenish the deficiency of the body (the acquired deficiency of vital essence, Qi and spirit as well as five types of strains and seven injuries) with the help of natural energy in the cosmos. The three Qigong exercises are made specially for replenishing the leaking body. For the patients who suffer from asthenic diseases, practicing the three Qigong exercises can cure their diseases; for Qigong practitioner the exercises can make them achieve an important breakthrough (sudden enlightenment) in Qigong; for those who are healthy mentally and physically the exercises can help them upgrade their health.

1. Gathering Sun Essence Exercise.

(1) Movement description.

Select a quiet open place with fresh air. Stand in a relaxed and tranquilized state while facing the sun (Fig. 15). Look at the sun one or two minutes (if the sunlight is too strong, close the eyes and have an inward view of it to avoid the sunlight injuring the eyes). Stretch the hands towards the sun as if to pick it down (Fig. 16) while softly breathing in one mouthful of Qi. Imagine you are picking the sun from the sky and holding it in front of the navel about five inches apart (Fig. 17). In your imagination the sun turns round gently by itself and makes your arms and body move with it. The key of the movement is that you must concentrate your mind on the thought that "the sun-ball is moving the hands and body" instead of "the hands are moving the ball." The movement of the whole body, including the hands, eyes, body, and steps, is flexible and natural (Figs. 18 and 19).

Fig. 15   Gathering Sun Essence Exercise (1)

Fig. 16　Gathering Sun Essence Exercise (2)

Fig. 17

Gathering Sun Essence
Exercise (3)

Gathering Sun Essence
Exercise (4)

Fig. 18

Fig. 19

Gathering Sun Essence
Exercise (5)

Fig. 20

Gathering Sun Essence
Exercise (6)

Fig. 21

Gathering Sun Essence
Exercise (7)

(2) Ending exercise.

Imagine that the "sun" in your arms moves slowly through the navel into the body. With the imagination, join the hands slowly with palms inward and place them on the navel, one hand on the other, accompanied by taking in a deep breathing (Fig. 20). Close the eyes and see inwards the sun beneath the navel becoming a golden illuminating ball. Taking in a deep breathing, imagine that the ball is spreading with each movement of exhalation to all parts of the body (Fig. 21). Then open the eyes, rub the hands and face, take a walk for a short while. This concludes the exercise.

(3) Frequency and duration of the exercise.

Once a day. One or two hours for each time.

For those with poor health more than once a day, but less than one hour for each time.

The best time for doing this Qigong exercise is within two hours after sun-rise. The time is different from place to place, from season to season. According to Traditional Chinese Medicine theory, the two hours after sun-rise is the best time in a day when there is sufficient "vital essence of the Sun," with Yang Qi rising and all things recovering and flourishing. Practicing the Qigong exercise at this time will bring more benefits to health.

(4) Points for attention.

a. Do not do this exercise inside the house.

b. Those who can not stand up must not practice it.

c. Do not practice it in cloudy days or when there is no Sun in the sky.

d. Do not mix it with other Qigong exercises.

(5) Function.

The Gathering Sun Essence Method has the function of gathering pure Yang-Qi and eliminating pathogenic factors, tonifying deficiency and consolidating the Essential Qi and preventing premature aging. *Huang-ting-jing* (*The Canon of Huang-ting*) says: "Sunlight and moonlight can prevent senescence." So practicing the Qigong is beneficial for those with poor health caused by Yang deficiency.

2. Gathering Moon Cream Exercise.

(1) Movement description.

a. At night when the moon is visible in the sky during the time from the eighth to the twenty-third day of the lunar month, select an open place and stand in a tranquilized state facing the moon (Fig. 22). Look at the moon (or with closed eyes) for about five minutes. Raise both arms to the front and imagine you were holding the moon in your hands (Fig. 23). While inhaling, raise both arms half a *chi* over the Baihui (No. 12) acupoint at the top of the head (Figs. 24 and 25); and then raise the arms and hold the moon half a *chi* in front of the Shanzhong acupoint (No. 3), and then half a *chi* in front of the Dantian point (Figs. 26 and 27). Close the eyes and imagine there were three moons over the top of the head, in front of the chest and of the Dantian separately. You may keep this imagination as long as you like.

b. Continuing from the previous exercise, raise the arms over the head. While inhaling, turn the palms downwards and imagine that the moon is pressed into the head through the Baihui point. At the same time hold the hands together with one over the other on the Baihui point for a while (Fig. 28). Then stretch both hands to the front of the body and turn the palms inward while imagining the moon in front of the Shanzhong point and that in front of the Dantian are brought into the body (Figs. 29, 30). The movement of hands must be accompanied by inhaling the air. Then imagine there are three moons under the Baihui, Shanzhong and Dantian separately. You can imagine it as long as you like.

c. Then tap at the Baihui point softly with the left hand (for male) or the right hand (for female). Imagine that with the tapping the three moons form a white pole of light in the center of the body (from the Baihui to the Huiyin point) (See No.16 on the Diagram of Acupoints). You can imagine it as long as you like (Figs. 31 to 33).

(2) Then open the eyes slowly and rub the hands together and rub the face with the hands. This concludes the exercise.

(3) Frequency and Duration of the Exercise.

Within the days prescribed above, once every night. Each time do it as long as you like to your needs.

Fig. 22
Gathering Moon Cream
Exercise (1)

Fig. 23   Gathering Moon Cream Exercise (2)

Fig. 24
Gathering Moon Cream
Exercise (3)

Fig. 25
Gathering Moon Cream
Exercise (4)

Fig. 26
Gathering Moon Cream
Exercise (5)

Gathering Moon Cream
Exercise (6)

Fig. 27

Fig. 28

Gathering Moon Cream
Exercise (7)

Fig. 29

Gathering Moon Cream
Exercise (8)

Fig. 30

Gathering Moon Cream
Exercise (9)

Fig. 31

Gathering Moon Cream
Exercise (10)

Fig. 32

Gathering Moon Cream
Exercise (11)

Gathering Moon Cream
Exercise (12)

Fig. 33

(4) Points for attention.

a. The principle for the imagination exercise is to do it in a relaxed and natural state. Do not demand the "scene" urgently.

b. Do not do the Qigong beyond the prescribed time (by lunar calendar from the 23rd day of a month to the 7th day of the next month).

c. Do not do the Qigong when the moon is covered by clouds.

(5) Efficacy.

Practicing the Qigong makes one take in moon cream (cool light) to nourish the kidney, keep the *jing* (the vital essence), strengthen the brain, accumulate the marrow, and achieve longevity.

3. Postnatal Development Exercise.

(1) Movement description.

Take a relaxed and quiescent form in standing posture. Clench both fists softly and put them at the waist (Fig. 34). The left foot takes a step forward and raise the right fist to the front slowly while bending over; beat the Yinbai acupoint (No.10) at the side of the left toenail with the right fist while exhaling naturally. Imagine there is Qi, with the movement of the right fist, going into the Yinbai point. At the end of the exhaling, the right fist is about one inch apart from the Yinbai point (The fist should suspend in the air. Do not touch the foot with the fist). The left fist is still at the waist and does not move. (Figs. 35, 36)

After finishing the above movement, draw back slowly the right fist and put it at the waist, inhaling naturally. Draw back the left foot and resume the standing posture (Fig. 34).

Then the right foot takes a step forward. Following the above exercise, beat the right Yinbai point with the left fist. Beat in this way the left and right Yinbai points alternatively. Repeat several times (Figs. 37, 38).

In doing the exercise, attention should be put on breathing naturally, and breath should coordinates with the movements, and the body should be relaxed. Do the movements gently and slowly; The eyes may be open or closed while doing the exercise.

(2) To end the exercise, put forward the foot lagging behind, stand with both feet on a line, close the eyes, place

Fig. 34
Postnatal Development
Exercise (1)

Fig. 35
Postnatal Development
Exercise (2)

Fig. 36

Postnatal Development
Exercise (3)

Fig. 37

Postnatal Development
Exercise (4)

Fig. 38

Postnatal Development
Exercise (5)

Fig. 39

Postnatal Development
Exercise (6)

both hands at the navel, visualize in the mind the navel, and rotate the hands on it several minutes. This brings the exercise to an end (Fig. 39).

(3) Frequency and duration of exercise.

Three to six times a day, 30-60 minutes each time.

(4) Effects.

Practicing the Qigong is beneficial for spleen and stomach as well as the concerned chronic diseases.

(5) Taboo.

The patients who suffer from schizophrenia, Meniere's syndrome, severe high blood pressure or heart disease, and who cannot bend the waist are recommended not to do the Qigong exercise.

(6) Points for attention.

a. In doing the exercise breath naturally, coordinate the movements, and relax the body.

b. You might feel a little dizzy at the beginning. This is caused by the fact that you did not breathe naturally or your movements were not soft and harmonious enough for the exercise. When you correct these, the dizziness will be got rid of.

c. You are recommended to do the Qigong in the open air in hot and cold seasons. It is beneficial for your health.

(7) Effects.

The training of breathing and gentle physical movement accompanied by the imagination of having the Qi passing into the Yinbai point have the function of making the pure Qi rise and the pathogenic Qi going down the body and making the postnatal essence, i.e. spleen essence, spread to all parts of the body. Thus practicing the Qigong can cure the diseases caused by imbalance between Yin and Yang and the asthenic diseases caused by maladjustment of postnatal essence. Because practicing the Qigong in the open air in the winter and summer has good effects, it is said: "The pure Qi replaces pathogenic Qi when the cold season alternates with the hot season."

The *Internal Canon of Medicine (Neijing)* says: "The spleen functions like the earth, from which everything grows and flourishes." Therefore, the Traditional Chinese Medicine attributes the maladjustment of postnatal essence to the spleen. For instance, the debility of the limbs is attributed to insufficiency of the nutrition supplied by the spleen because "the spleen governs the limbs"; neurasthenia is attributed to excessive worry, which suppresses the spleen's function (because the spleen governs the emotional system). For the Chinese medicine it is significant to nourish the postnatal essence and strengthen the function of spleen and stomach. The key function of the Qigong exercise is to stimulate the start point of the spleen channel, the Yinbai acupoint, to nourish the postnatal essence and strengthen the function of spleen and stomach. Besides, it can also help the practitioner to improve his mood for static Qigong, to get rid of restlessness and jumpy mood, and to concentrate the mind. According to the Traditional Chinese Medicine theory, the spleen is the storage of emotions. Sufficient spleen essence will lead to healthy mental state, with which one can easily concentrate the mind and achieve a tranquilized mood.

III. The Qigong for Prolonging Life
   (*Dong Tian Shou Bao Gong*)

This Qigong exercise is a secretly kept method of medical circles and it has never been put down in written records. It has only passed down from master to disciples orally. Many doctors of traditional Chinese medicine of older generations have been benefited from it. This Qigong exercise has been popularized during recent years and it is proved that it can exploit the potential energy of the body, cure chronic diseases, and delay the process of aging.

This Qigong exercise is easy to learn and practice. It has no taboos and won't cause side-effects, and so it is a good means of combating aging and prolonging life. It is especially good for those who suffer from chronic mental depression and who are of weak physical constitution, and for those whose family members had a record of short life.

The method consists of three steps. The first step can mobilize the brain's potential energy to cure diseases and prolong life; the second step gives a happy mood to eliminate liver stasis and bad mood, which is important for prolonging life; the third step, called *Wu-fu-zeng-shou-shi* (the posture that can produce five happiness and prolong life) because it stimulates directly the Shanzhong acupoint (also called "Sea of Qi" by Chinese physicians, see No.3 on the Diagram of Acupoints) at the center of the chest, can tonify Qi and strengthen the essence and prolong life.

Movement Description.

1. Take a comfortable sitting posture. Close the eyes slightly. Relax the body. Imagine slightly there is white mist around the head with the back of the head as its center and the diameter of the mist is about a meter long. The duration of the imagination is not limited. The key point is that you should not concentrate your mind strenuously and you should relax your whole body.

2. Take the same sitting posture. Close the eyes slightly. No longer imagine the white mist. Slightly cover the

navel with both hands. (You may cover the navel from outside the clothes.) Relax the body. Strike slightly both sides of the body with the elbows (do not move the hands away from the navel). Inhale while the elbows are up; exhale while they are down. Breath softly. The breathing should coordinate with the movement of the elbows. Repeat the strike until you exhale 30 times. But a practitioner with weak constitution may do less than 30 times if he feels tired.

3. Take the same sitting posture. Cross the fingers of both hands with finger tips touching the other hand's finger roots, both thumbs put together side by side and both palms inward facing each other, just like making a bow with hands folded in front. Place the hands in front of the center of the chest, three inches apart from the Shanzhong acupoint. Close the eyes. Relax the body. Do not have any idea in the mind. The method is called *Wu-fu-zeng-shou-gong.* The duration of this exercise is not limited. Do it as long as you like each time. The ending of the third step is also the conclusion of this Qigong exercise.

IV. Initial Method for the Supreme Qigong

Sheng-xu-he-dao-gong (Exercise for Unifying the Mindwill and Qi)

1. Introduction.

For practicing this Qigong practitioners are required to have a thorough understanding of its theory and to make a deep-going mental work. The Qigong exercise is flexible and simple, and is easy to learn. Once you have learned the ABC of this Qigong, you can get to a higher stage, the "true realm" of "unification of mindwill and Qi," and finally reach the highest stage, the "realm of emptiness and nature" by way of practising both Qigong and morality as well as cultivating both nature and body. The method here is of a higher grade. So the starting point is of high level. The practitioners are required to combine at once the mind with the state of *Xu* (Emptiness), which leads directly to Supreme Qigong.

The most important thing for practicing the Supreme Qigong is to have a correct dominant idea. What method you follow is secondary. Besides, an enterprising spirit in practicing it and a correct understanding of its theory are also necessary.

In practicing the Supreme Qigong one should follow the principle of being "non-active and natural." The practitioners are not required to follow consciously the "three regulations (of the body, breathing and mind)" or "three trainings," nor are they asked to pay much attention on the "three Dantians" and the "three passes and nine keys." But it does not mean that they do not need to "regulate" or "train," or to give play to the functions of the "three Dantians" and the "three passes and nine keys." Instead, they should lead them go naturally. The Qigong should be done with "genuine intention" as the *Internal Canon of Medicine* (*Neijing*) teaches. The so-called "genuine intention" is referred to "without intention." Therefore, success can be attained and the skill and energy will show up unintentionally with a subtle influence, just as it is put in a Chinese saying: "You plant willows unintentionally but the willow grows very well."

2. Posture description.

A beginner can take any one of the following three postures: lying, sitting or standing. However, in order to lay a sound basis for further training and have a persisting training in a tranquilized condition, he is recommended to take a sitting posture with crossed legs and with both soles of the feet upward. For the male, place the left leg on the right; for the female, the right leg on the left. Place both hands, one on the other, (for the male, the left hand on the right; for the female, the right hand on the left) below the navel, with palms upward, fingers slightly separated and thumbs one inch apart from each other. (Fig. 1)

Adopt an upright sitting position with the head, neck and spine upright. Relax the body.

3. Method description.

Drop the eyelids slightly or look at the nose with half-closed eyes. Imagine unintentionally that the navel becomes a golden ring of light. Keep the imagination for a quarter of an hour. Then forget yourself and all things. This is the beginning of the Qigong exercise. The key method is "to be non-active." Give up all thoughts and let your mind fall into a trance. If thoughts emerge in your mind, do not try to eliminate them, nor worry about them. Instead, let them go away by themselves. Keep "Sambodhi" (the wisdom of a Buddha) and the "genuine intention" in a tranquilized state when sitting (or standing or lying). For practicing this style of Qigong there is no limitation of time, but a long meditation will surely lead to *Chan*.

4. Ending exercise.

To end the Qigong practice means to give up the posture of practicing it. However, you must not have the idea of ending it in your mind, in which lies the difference between the Qigong method and the others. Thus you can easily preserve the Qigong condition in daily activities and attain good results. This will lay a good foundation for practicing the Qigong all day long.

5. Points for attention.

(1) People who are not used to crossing legs may have a pain in the waist and legs. Then strike slightly the waist and legs with both hollow fists until the pain is lessened. While you do it, you can stretch or cross your legs, close or open your eyes. After that go on with the exercise.

(2) People who do the meditation only for curing diseases and health care need not cross the legs. They may take a simple sitting or other postures.

Those who find it difficult to cross the legs may take the natural cross-legged sitting posture or single cross-legged sitting posture before they become used to the crossed legged sitting posture. Making the single cross-legged sitting posture, men and women are different in the position of legs. The requirement is the same as in the cross-legged posture.

(3) The Qigong meditation has no side effects or taboo diseases.

(4) You can do the meditation under any condition, no matter whether you are hungry or full or tired.

(5) Practitioners of higher level can always keep the Qigong state during the day-time, even when sleeping. This the beginners are difficult to understand, but they will experience it when they are good at the exercise.

V. The Qigong for Emitting the Qi (*Pu-zhao-bu-qi-gong*): Basic Exercise and Application Qigong

1. Introduction.

This is an introduction of a traditional exercise for emitting the Qi. The exercise is significant for the doctors who emit the Qi to cure diseases.

This Qigong exercise is characterized by that the Qi can be quickly felt by the practitioner. So it is quite effective in curing one's own disease or other people's disease. This Qigong exercise has a long history, and it is easy to practice. One can practice it for the treatment of one's as well as other people's disease. It proves to have excellent clinical effects, especially on chronic diseases. Thus it is significant for physicians to learn for clinical practice.

2. Theory.

The aim of "the Qigong for Emitting the Qi" is to lay a foundation for facilitating the flow of information between the practitioner and cosmos and for getting energy from the nature to meet the needs of human body ("small cosmos"), and therefore a practitioner should not use it for clinical practice before he has done the basic exercise earnestly for one hundred days.

The clinical application of this Qigong is one of the important skills to use "external Qi" to cure diseases.

The Qigong information has the characteristics of life, ideology, movement, holography, objective, two-way, super-distance, comprehension, flexibility, distinction, penetration, surmounting selection, regional nature, transmission, reclamation, accumulation, automatic nature, auto-compensation, and not decreasing with the changes of time and space, etc.

Therefore, the Qigong of emitting Qi can make Qigong masters improve their medical skills and also can reinforce body power to eliminate pathogens. So it can cure diseases and strengthen health. There is no conflict between this Qigong and other kinds of Qigong. They can promote each other's effectiveness so far as they are not practiced at the same time or are mixed together.

3. Basic Exercise.

(1) Preparation: Stand in a relax and tranquilized state. Draw back the chin a little. Slightly close the eyes. Stay in the meditation state for fifteen minutes. (Fig. 5)

(2) Start the exercise: As this Qigong exercise can be done with eyes open or closed, the sense of Qi felt varies from person to person. Thus, whether to do the exercise with eyes open or closed will be decided by the practitioner himself. He should do it with the method in which he can easily sense the Qi.

Place both hands half *chi* (a unit of length, =1/3 meter) in front of the navel, palms facing each other. Imagine that the hands are holding a red fire-ball as big as a basketball. Rotate the ball from the back to the front and imagine the ball is being rotated quickly by the hands. (Note: It is done in the same manner as you turn a globe with your hands. When you turn it slightly, the globe will turn round quickly.) Do the exercise for five minutes.

(3) Afterwards, do the exercise in the opposite direction. Rotate the fire-ball from the front to the back and imagine that the fire-ball is turning round in the same direction as your hands are moving. Do it also for five minutes. (Fig. 40)

(4) Change to another hand gesture. Place one hand over the other, with palms facing each other. For men the left hand is over the right one; for women, vise versa. Imagine the ball is turning round and round quickly clockwise between your hands for five minutes and then in the opposite direction for another five minutes. (Fig. 41)

(5) Resume the starting gesture, placing the hands in front of the navel with palms facing each other. They are holding the fire-ball. Imagine that the hands are pressing slowly the ball into the navel, and at the same time the hands press in slowly toward the navel. (Fig. 42) When the palms touch the navel (Fig. 43), imagine that the fire-ball has gone into it. And then, imagine the ball in

the navel was slowly changing into golden rays of light spreading to all parts of the body.

(6) Raise both hands in front of the chest, shoulder width, with palms upward. Relax the body, including the shoulders and the waist. Imagine that abundant Qi from the heaven including various energy from cosmos such as rays, waves, and light was coming through the palms into the body (no matter along what route it moves into the body). Imagine the Qi keeps on coming into the body. (At the same time try to have the sense of Qi in order to choose appropriate time, place and direction for doing the exercise.) The exercise takes about ten minutes. (Fig. 44)

(7) Hold out both hands at both sides of the body, with palms downward, and hold out both feet apart. Imagine that the "earth Qi" energy such as terrestrial magnetism, heat of the earth's interior, subterranean radiation and light are coming upwards from the depth of the earth through the palms of hands into the body, and the pathogenic Qi is going downwards from the body's interior through the soles into the earth. The exercise takes about ten minutes. (Fig. 45)

Fig. 40

The Qigong for Emitting the Qi (*Pu-zhao-bu-qi-gong*) (1)

Fig. 41

The Qigong for Emitting the Qi (*Pu-zhao-bu-qi-gong*) (2)

Fig. 42

The Qigong for Emitting the
Qi *(Pu-zhao-bu-qi-gong)* (3)

Fig. 43

The Qigong for Emitting the
Qi *(Pu-zhao-bu-qi-gong)* (4)

Fig. 44

The Qigong for Emitting the
Qi *(Pu-zhao-bu-qi-gong)* (5)

Fig. 45

The Qigong for Emitting the
Qi *(Pu-zhao-bu-qi-gong)* (6)

(8) To end the exercise you are required only to take a walk for a while.

(9) Frequency and duration of exercise: The Qigong medical workers who give clinical treatment by means of Qigong such as emitting Qi, Qigong massage, Qigong acupuncture, Qigong fluoroscopy, and Qigong information water, should do the exercise once in the morning and evening separately to make up the consumption of Qi and get rid of evil information such as pathogenic Qi.

For practitioners who use Qigong to cure other people's diseases, should do it no less than three times a day.

For health protection do it once a day.

4. The Application Qigong.

The Application Qigong has no restriction on the posture, form, times, and frequency. It should be taken according to the actual condition. The best choice is to enhance the treatment efficiency. The practitioner should combine giving clinical treatment (for others) and self-training (for oneself) together to benefit the patient and himself. The following are eight methods of the Application Qigong.

(1) The "Exchange" Method.

By means of imagination the practitioner makes an "exchange" of the various parts of his body, or exchanges his body for the object that has nature information. The "exchange" may be accompanied by the movement of one hand or both hands.

Through the exchange of his body for the patient's body, the practitioner is able to know the patient's disease. (But those who do not have a solid foundation in the Qigong practice are not recommended to do the "exchange" so as to avoid side effects.)

The method can restore positive functions, replenish energy, and can help give clinical treatment by way of finding out what disease the patient suffers from.

(2) The Method of the "Regulation of Qi".

The method is to gather various Qi (information, energy, etc.) with the help of the mindwill. The concrete method should be taken in accordance with local conditions, the time, and the person concerned. The practitioner is recommended to take advantage of the movement of hands or the mindwill or subconsciousness—original spirit. In a word, what method a practitioner is to take should be decided by how much he had attained in the Qigong practice.

The method can be used to treat diseases. For instance, for the cold syndrome it is advisable to use the warming method: use such hot energy as sunlight, lamplight, fire-light, and electricity to eliminate the cold syndrome. For hot syndrome, it is advisable to use sea-water, ice or even liquid nitrogen to eliminate it. For the superficial and mild illness it is advisable to gather the drugs of relieving the illness as well as the smell of the drugs. For the treatment of concretion, the practitioner may gather some drugs in his mindwill to remove the stone. For a big stone it is advisable to gather laser. In a word, the method has rich content. Applying the method in medical treatment, the practitioner is required to have "Qigong consciousness," and be courageous enough to think and act, otherwise he will not succeed.

(3) The Method of Accumulating Qi.

The method is aimed to supply energy for the patients suffering from the deficiency syndrome. When applying the method, concentrate the mind on any Qi beneficial for the patients and supply it to them. For instance, for the patients suffering from deficiency of lung-Qi the practitioner may accumulate in his mindwill drugs good for the lung or anion to nourish the lung; for the patients suffering from deficiency of liver-Qi the drugs of nourishing the liver and kidney or the vitality of plants may be accumulated; for those suffering from neurasthenia and insomnia, moonlight or sea-water may be accumulated to calm them down.

The difference between the accumulation of Qi and the regulation of Qi is that the former's key point is "accumulation," the practitioner compressing energy to put its positive role into full play. It seems as if the mindwill compresses the energy in order to reinforce the efficacy of making up the deficiency.

(4) The Method of Seizing the Qi.

The method is aimed at curing diseases by way of

eliminating the evil Qi. The practitioner concentrates his mind on that his hand has seized the evil Qi and grabs it out of the patient's body. The method is beneficial for the diseases of "stagnation owing to excess of evil Qi" (the *Internal Canon of Medicine*).

(5) The Method of Discharging Evil Qi.

Imagine that your mindwill has gone into the patient's body to discharge the evil Qi from the inside to the outside. It can be accompanied by the movement of fingers, palms, or eyes or by breathing. It can be done only with the mindwill. The method is beneficial for the treatment of excess of evil Qi and disorders of Qi mechanism.

(6) The method of Dispersing the Qi.

Imagine that your mindwill disperses the evil Qi out of the patient's body. It is beneficial for curing minor diseases at the upper part of the body such as indigestion, loss of appetite, diseases caused by six external factors of the nature, and minor infectious diseases such as trachoma.

(7) The Method of Reflection.

Imagine the palm, a piece of paper, a fan, or any other thing as a reflector that can send by way of reflection all natural messages and energy from far and near into the body of the patient to cure his disease. The method is simple and convenient, and is quick in proving effective.

(8) The Method of Gathering Qi.

When using this method, the mind, hands and breathing are put into use synchronically. This is an important method of supplying energy before and after emitting external Qi (*waiqi*) to treat diseases. The Qi of the plant is usually gathered to supply energy for the human body. The method is as follows: when inhaling, concentrate the mind on gathering the Qi, and the hands doing gestures of gathering the Qi and taking it back. The three steps should be done in harmony and synchronically. As to where to put the Qi or where to put the withdrawn hands it can be decided according to the practitioner's needs. Usually the place is where the Qi is sent out, such as the palm of hand, the three *Guans* (passes) and the nine *Qiao* (key points) and other sensitive parts of the body.

However, the Qi one takes to enrich his energy must be from the nature instead of other people. Otherwise it will be immoral, nor will it benefit him, because one should not absorb other people's Qi. It can be explained with the theory of exclusiveness such as the medical theory of exclusiveness of the protein of different race. The Qi and protein, though different in form, are of the same category of substances. So the same theory can be applied to the Qi. In fact one cannot in any case keep another person's Qi in one's body, because the foreign Qi will be expelled. Besides, to take other people's Qi will be harmful to oneself, because in excluding the foreign Qi one has to suffer the loss of his own energy. Is it a gain or a loss? I think, to take morality seriously is real gains.

5. Points for Attention.

(1) The direction and place for the Qigong training must not be fixed and unchangeable. When condition permits, you should change the direction and place so as to find out the direction and place where you can get the strongest Qi sensation, and you should change the direction and place in time according to the changes of the Qi sensation. Only by this way you can improve the effects of the emission of Qi and boost the energy.

(2) The Application Qigong should be done on the basis of Basic Exercise. Nobody should use the Application Qigong without proper training of the Basic Exercise. For a healthy person, no matter whether he has learned Qigong of other schools or not, he may do the Application Qigong after a hundred days of serious training in the Basic Exercise. After a month or so, he may try to emit eternal Qi to treat diseases. Afterwards, he may decide his clinical therapeutic scope according to his own power of emitting of external Qi.

(3) The eight methods of the Application Qigong are only fundamental methods. Practitioners should bring these methods into full play and practice them elastically; they should not rigidly adhere to the detailed procedures.

(4) As the practitioners can absorb comprehensive, high-energy materials with this Qigong, a few beginners

may feel a bit unwell temporarily. This is a normal phenomenon, indicating that a preliminary connection between them and the Nature—cosmos—has been established. The way of dispelling the discomfort is as follows: beat slightly the front and the outer side of the legs above the knees. Continue to do the exercise after the discomfort disappears. If the discomfort reoccurs, repeat the leg-beating movement until the discomfort completely disappears.

(5) It is a good thing that pathology appears owing to Qigong exercises. Don't worry about it. But you should not be impatient to emit outer Qi. Cure your own diseases first. You can cure others only when you have strengthened yourself.

(6) This Qigong is a dynamic Qigong, so it is advisable to do it among trees, flowers and green crops, which can give out flourishing Qi, when the climate is suitable.

VI. The Qigong for Women

This Qigong pattern is specifically for women according to women's physical characteristics. It puts stress on the regulation of the Qi mechanism of the Chong and Ren channels to meet women's physical needs. It is an important Qigong exercise for keeping good health and curing diseases, especially women's diseases.

The Qigong consists of two methods as follows:

1. *Kun-shun-sheng-hua-gong* (Women's Recuperating-life Qigong)

(1) Introduction.

Women are recommended to do the *Kun-shun-sheng-hua-gong* during the time of about 40 years from the beginning of menstruation at about 7 years of age to the menopause at about 49, because the Qigong is beneficial for their physical and mental health and it can make them fresh with vigor.

The Qigong is especially good for women with chronic diseases. It also helps the recovery of health for women after childbirth.

(2) Method

Assuming a kneeling posture. Kneel with both knees on a soft mat, with upright waist, drawn-in chest, upright head, relaxed body and slightly closed eyes (Figs. 46, 47). Place both hands at the back of the body at the bottom of the spine, with the left hand holding the four fingers (except the thumb) of the right hand (Fig. 48). The method can regulate the Qi mechanism of *Chong* and *Ren* Channels, which are thought to be the key points for the regulation of Qi of women. Thus to take a kneeling posture is very important for the method.

Having assumed the posture, breathe naturally. While breathing out, read silently (but the lips-position and tongue position will be the same as that when you read them out aloud) the following words, each time a word in this order: *ding, dang, di, du,* and *duan*. When you read each one of the words, imagine that the Qi comes out from the Shanzhong acupoint (No.3) down to the Dantian point at about four fingers below the navel.

While inhaling, do not read any one of the words and do not make the imagination. The five words will be read in the exact order, one for taking an exhaling, change to the next word when making the next exhaling. Altogether read every word three times.

After reading the words three times, continue to assume the kneeling posture and breathe naturally with slightly closed eyes. Place both hands with palms at the kidney Shenshu acupoint (No. 13 on the Diagram of Acupoints) on the waist (see Fig. 49). Imagine the pungent smell of ginger, Chinese prickly ash, and pepper going through the navel into the *Dantian* area below the navel, where it becomes as sweet as the smell of flowers, fruit, or plant (for instance, sandalwood), or of animals (for instance, musk). Imagine that the sweet smell is stored in the area of *Dantian*, and then try to appreciate the fragrance in your imagination.

(3) Ending Exercise

To conclude the exercise, take a deep breathing and imagine the "sweet smell" at the *Dantian* spreading to all

Fig. 46
Women's Recuperating-Life Qigong *(Kun-shun-sheng-hua-gong)* (1)

Fig. 47
Women's Recuperating-Life Qigong *(Kun-shun-sheng-hua-gong)* (2)

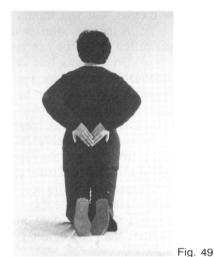

Fig. 48

Fig. 49

Women's Recuperating-Life Qigong *(Kun-shun-sheng-hua-gong)* (3)

Women's Recuperating-Life Qigong *(Kun-shun-sheng-hua-gong)* (4)

parts of the body including the tips of limbs and the head. Keep the imagination for three or five minutes and then slowly open the eyes, rub the hands and face, thus ending the exercise.

(4) Frequency and duration of the exercise.

As to how long you should take the kneeling posture, it may be decided in accordance with your health conditions. Conclude the exercise when you feel tired. Do not struggle to continue it. Otherwise you will be overtired. The greater attainment you get, the longer you can practice it.

A patient is recommended to do it several times a day, but each time for a short while.

For health protection it is advisable to do it twice a day, each time for half an hour.

(5) Points for attention

a. A healthy woman may imagine the sweet smell coming through the navel into the Dantian instead of the pungent smell of ginger, Chinese prickly ash, and pepper coming into it.

b. It will be more effective to do it during the period

of menses, but you should never be overtired by going it.

c. A person who is or was a schizophrenic is not permitted to do the exercise.

d. Do not mix this exercise with *Zhi-fa-gong* (spontaneous expression of feelings owing to the practice of Qigong). Do not do this training exercise and other Qigong maneuvers at the same time, except the Qigong maneuvers introduced in this book; there should be at least two hours' separation between them.

e. To practice the Qigong for a long period of time will make the practitioner be full of vigor. But do not practice it during the period from 3 months pregnancy to child-birth.

f. The practitioner may do this exercise no matter whether she is a beginner or has had some experience in Qigong.

g. The experience of the pepper smell and the sweet smell varies from person to person. The practitioner should not pursue a certain kind of smell. The main point is to relax the body and relieve the mind, and let things go naturally.

h. After practicing the maneuver for a period of time, some people will have a sweet smell emitting out of their bodies, and they themselves or other people can sense it. Although it is a good phenomenon of Qigong training, we shall neither suspect it nor insist on seeking for it. Let it take its own course.

i. It is good to practice it before the first menses and after the menopause. The method is beneficial to health protection, but it cannot make a woman strong and beautiful.

2. *Bao-yang-tai-yuan-fa*
(Qigong for protecting the fetus)

(1) Introduction

This Qigong maneuver is good for women suffering from habitual abortion. It can protect the embryo from abortion. It can also prevent the habitual abortion.

(2) Method

You may assume any posture. Slightly close the eyes; relax the body, and breathe naturally.

Imagine there is a red flower (any red flower that you like best, for instance, lotus flower or rose) inside your lower abdomen. While inhaling, imagine the flower going out through the abdomen wall and rising up to a certain height in the sky. When the inhaling ended, imagine the flower staying in the air. While exhaling, concentrate the mind on the flower. While inhaling again, imagine the red flower rising up from its original place in the sky. Do exercise like this for 3 or 5 minutes. Afterwards, pay no attention to the breathing; only imagine the red flower staying high in the air and flashing out golden light three times. Each time it emits golden light, concentrate your mind on the flower for about three minutes. After it has flashed golden light three times, bring the exercise to an end.

(3) Ending exercise.

Slowly open the eyes, rub the palms of the hands till they become warm, then rub the top of the head and the forehead with the palms until they also become warm.

(4) Frequency and duration of the exercise.

During gestational period do the exercise three times a day, each time for fifteen minutes.

The Qigong exercise is beneficial for women suffering from habitual abortion. The exercise can lay a good foundation for the pregnant women.

(5) Indication

The exercise is useful for the women who has a history of habitual abortion and who had occasional abortion once or twice.

(6) Taboo

The women who should stop pregnancy.

(7) Points for attention

a. Breath naturally. Never breath in with a force.

b. Relax the body and the mind.

c. Practicing this Qigong maneuver will never cause a difficult labour.

d. This Qigong maneuver has the function of correcting the wrong position of fetus.

VII. The Qigong for Children

Introduction

The Medical Qigong for Children is good for children and teen-agers. It is based on the medical experiences by physicians of older generations and is a basic method of Qigong training of children.

The following are two important maneuvers.

This Qigong is good for children of various ages and various physical conditions. It has been shown through practice that the Qigong exercise can improve the physical and mental health of children and young people and can cure some common diseases of children. It can also cure partiality for a particular kind of food, loss of appetite, physical underdevelopment, poor resistance against disease, myopia, as well as the diseases caused by overburden in study, such as neurasthenia, insomnia, dreaminess, menstrual irregularities, and disturbance of the spleen and stomach. It helps to overcome such troubles with children as willfulness and impatience and can foster the children's strong will and vigorous health.

1. *Da-zhi-gong*
   (The Qigong for Improving Intellectual Faculties)

   (1) Maneuver
   a. Assume any posture. Relax the body. Do the exercise with eyes open or closed. Raise the hands. Place the left hand, for the male, or the right hand, for the female, at about three inches from the Yintang acupoint (No. 1) at the forehead with the palm inwards facing the acupoint, and the other hand at the same level with the palm outwards. The two hands at the same level are three inches apart from each other with the two outward Laogong acupoints (No. 8) facing each other. Make a clockwise cyclical movement of the two hands with the Yintang acupoint as its center. Do it for several minutes. Then move slowly both hands to the front of the right eye and make the same movement with the right eye as its center. Then move slowly the hands to the front of the left eye and do the same movement. After that, do the

same movement again in front of the forehead with the Yintang acupoint as its center. As to how long a practitioner will do the movement, it may be decided by himself (see Figs. 50 and 51).

b. Place both hands each at half a *chi* from the external ear with the Laogong point facing the ear-hole. Move both hands (forward or backward) in the same direction synchronously. Do not concentrate your mind. Breathe naturally (see Fig. 52).

c. Touch the navel with the middle-finger of one hand and the Mingmen (No. 14) point with that of another hand. Touch them slightly (Fig. 53). Imagine there was a big red fire ball in the abdomen between the two middle-fingers till you feel warm in the abdomen. (If it becomes too hot, breathing out with open mouth and reading out the word "Ha" three times to release the heat.)

(2) Ending exercise.

Cover the tail bone with both hands and jump gently for several minutes. Do not concentrate the mind. As to how high and how fast you jump, it is to your needs. Do not get tired from the jumping (Fig. 54).

Fig. 50

The Qigong for Improving Intellectual Faculties
(Da-zhi-gong) (1)

Fig. 51   The Qigong for Improving Intellectual Faculties *(Da-zhi-gong)* (2)

Fig. 52   The Qigong for Improving Intellectual Faculties *(Da-zhi-gong)* (3)

Fig. 53

Fig. 54

The Qigong for Improving
Intellectual Faculties
(Da-zhi-gong) (4)

The Qigong for Improv-
ing Intellectual Faculties
(Da-zhi-gong) (5)

(3) Points for attention.

a. The Qigong is good for children 3 to 12 years old.

b. The children with weak constitution or suffer from serious diseases, or have difficulty in standing up should not do this Qigong maneuver.

c. The time and frequency of the Qigong practice are not fixed. Children had better to practice it diligently.

d. Remind the children that they should relax the body and mind when doing the exercise.

e. Do the whole process of the Qigong exercise. Do it in sequence. Do not practice only a part of it. Do not reverse the order of the exercise.

2. *Tong-ling-gong* (The Qigong for Gaining Wisdom)

(1) Maneuver.

Stand with feet flat and spaced as wide as shoulder width. Cover with one hand the lower Dantian below the navel and with another hand the part at the back waist (below the Mingmen point) opposite the lower Dantian. Close the eyes and relax the body and mind for three minutes. Imagine that the upper part of the body above the waist is in the blue sky and below it are clouds and you yourself have changed into a very big *Sun-wu-kong*, the Monkey King (Figs. 55, 56). Imagine the figure of *Sun-wu-kong* freely. Put your imagination into full play. The imagination should be accompanied by the movement of both legs, gently trembling with knees as the center.

(2) Points for attention.

a. This Qigong exercise is good for children of 3 to 16.

b. Do the exercise in the open air.

c. The time and frequency of the exercise may be decided by the practitioner himself.

d. Conclude the exercise in any form.

e. There is no taboo for this Qigong maneuver.

Fig. 55

The Qigong for Gaining
Wisdom *(Tong-ling-gong)* (1)

Fig. 56

The Qigong for Gaining
Wisdom *(Tong-ling-gong)* (2)

VIII. The Folk Qigong of the Medical School

Mu-yu-jing-shen-gong (The Qigong of Taking a Bath to Clean the Body)

1. Introduction

This Qigong was passed down by physicians of older generations. Through long-term practice the Qigong proves to be effective. We would like to recommend it to Qigong-practitioners. Its main methods are as follows.

2. Maneuvers

(1) Dew Drops Falling on the Head (*Gan-lu-guan-ding*).

Relax the body. Slightly close the eyes. Assume any posture. Imagine that above the head is the sky, wide and cloudless. Be relaxed and happy. Keep the imagination for a quarter of an hour.

Then, imagine that the blue sky is full of dew drops as crystal-clear and sparkling as those on lotus leaves. Then imagine that the dew drops are falling down on your head and from your head down into your body, and that the whole body is being washed with a large amount of dew drops, from the top to the bottom and from the inside to the outside. Imagine that with the washing the pathogenic Qi is driven out, going down out from the soles and toes into the ground. Do the imagination and wash yourself with dew drops three times.

(2) Being reborn by changing bones (*Tuo-tai-huan-gu*).

Following the previous exercise, continue your imagination with the same method and posture as mentioned above. Imagine that with the dew drops covering the whole body the bones separated from each other, beginning with the tail bone, followed by the backbones, shoulder blades, and skull, all of which dropped out of the body in a stream following the tail-bone.

Then imagine that the bones of both feet and hands also dropped in a stream out of the body, through the soles and toes into the ground. So did the bones of both hands and both sides. They all dropped out of the body through the feet. After all the bones of the body dropped out, gently move the body several time and imagine the crystal-clear dew drops being evenly distributed in the body.

(3) Clean the body with three baths (*San-yu-jing-shen*).

The three baths refer to being bathed in sunlight, wind and rain by means of imagination. The basic principle and posture are the same as the above. However, do the exercise when the weather is appropriate.

a. Sunlight bathing.

Continuing from the previous exercise, do the exercise outdoors when it is fine. Slightly close the eyes. Imagine that the body has become as transparent as glass and crystal, and the sun threw its warm light through it. The time for the exercise is not limited. This Qigong exercise may vitalize the Yang-Qi.

b. Rain bathing.

Follow the "Tuo-tai-huan-gu" method. Do the exercise indoors when it is raining. Slightly close the eyes. Imagine that the body becomes vacant and the rain drops come into the body without resistance, and the rain cleans the inside of the body. Don't do this Qigong exercise when the thunder rolls. The time for the exercise is not limited. This exercise is good for the Yin-Qi.

c. Wind bathing.

Follow the "Tuo-tai-huan-gu" method. Do this exercise when it is windy. For those who are of poor health and when there is strong wind, it is advisable to do it indoors. Otherwise, do it outdoors. Slightly close the eyes; imagine that the wind blows through the body and blows the pathogenic Qi and turbid Qi out of it. The time for doing it is not limited. The exercise can regulate Yin and Yang of the body.

3. Applications

(1) This Qigong exercise is beneficial for those who suffer from deficiency of Qi and blood, disharmony between Yin and Yang caused by impairment of the viscera, and deficiency of the primordial Qi, diseases called in modern medicine as neurasthenia and neurosis.

(2) This exercise is also beneficial for the treatment of various bone diseases such as osteoporosis, osteomyelitis, anostosis, osteoarthritis, tuberculosis of bones and joints, etc.

(3) This exercise can raise up the Pure Qi and bring down the turbid Qi, so by means of it the Qigong master can rapidly remove the illness Qi he accidentally absorbed from the patient during clinical treatment.

(4) This exercise can fill up the deficiency of Qi and strengthen the primary force of activities of life.

IX. Advanced Qigong Exercises

Wu-zang-wai-jing-gong (Qigong of an External View of the Viscera)

1. Introduction

The Qigong of an External View of the Viscera is a maneuver based on the Qigong of an Internal View of the Viscera. So, the former can be practiced only after the latter has been done for at least a hundred days. Otherwise, the training cannot bring out the desired results.

2. Posture

It is better to assume a sitting posture, facing the south, though one can also assume a standing posture. Do not assume a lying posture. The basic principles of this Qigong training are the same as those of the Qigong of Internal View of the Viscera.

3. Method.

Slightly close the eyes. Relax and tranquilize yourself. After several minutes imagine that at the back, in the north, is a vast dark ocean. The ocean and the back of your body seem to fuse together. Wait until the scene in the imagination becomes clear (it will take several minutes). Then imagine that the left side, in the east, is an immense dense forest, which seem to join together with the left side of the body. (The forest has various trees, mainly pines. You may imagine different trees at different times.) When the scene becomes clearer, make the following imagination. Imagine that in front of the body, in the south, are great "fire mountains," on which are only flames, but without any smoke. (Pay attention to this point.) When the scene becomes clear, imagine that your body has become a "loess mound" with fine yellowish soil.

From then on, forget your own body and replace it with the "loess mound" in your imagination. Then imagine that at the right side of the mound, in the west, the ground is covered with glistening platinum. (It doesn't matter what form the platinum is.) Wait until the scene becomes clear. After that let the five scenes co-exist in your imagination and forget yourself in the Qigong state. As to how long you would keep the state, it is according to your needs. The Qigong state is important for the appearance of Qigong energy and the development of potential energy in the body. Thus, the more to practice it, the better.

4. Conclude the training.

Think that you are to close the training, and then bring yourself from the Qigong state of the five scenes to reality. Open the eyes. Rub both hands until they become warm. Rub the face with the palms of the hands for several minutes. Then do the following exercises:

(1) Patients are recommended to stroke and rub the the part of the body that is the focus of disease with the palms of the hands. The length of time for the self-massage should be decided according to their health conditions. A patient suffering from chronic diseases should do it 15-20 minutes each time, and every time apply massage to two sick parts (one at the right side and the other at the left side). If there are more than two foci of diseases, apply massage to two each time alternately. The method is good for self-treatment of disease (Fig. 57).

(2) A person in good health or with experiences of Qigong practice, in order to strengthen his Qigong energy, is recommended to give stimulation to some important points of his body such as Dantian, Mingmen, and Yongquan, some acupoints on the head, and some sensitive points at the eyes, ears and armpits.

The method is as follows: do the movement of pushing, drawing, opening and closing with both palms or one palm on one or two sick points each time. While doing the movement of closing, do not touch either the skin of the body or the clothing; while doing the movement of opening, the hand will not be more than two *chi* from the body. Do not make any imagination. The time for the Qigong exercise is under the control of the practitioner himself. To do the Qigong day after day will increase Qigong efficacy and strengthen body energy (Figs. 58 and 59).

After doing the whole exercise, rub the hands and the

Fig. 57

Qigong of an External View of
the Viscera
(Wu-zang-wai-jing-gong) (1)

Fig. 58

Qigong of an External View of
the Viscera
(Wu-zang-wai-jing-gong) (2)

Fig. 59

Qigong of an External View of
the Viscera *(Wu-zang-wai-jing-gong)* (3)

face and then move the feet for several minutes. The way
for moving the feet is as follows: moving the toes and
then the soles of the feet. Lay stress on the "movement of
toes." This concludes the Qigong exercise.

5. The frequency and duration of the exercise.

(1) To cure diseases do it three times a day.

(2) To enhance body functions do it 1-2 times a day.

(3) For those who practice Qigong temporarily, no limitation is made on the number of times and the length of time.

(4) The two methods for ending the Qigong exercise can be practiced independently without the precedent practice of the External View of the Viscera. For this no limitation is made on the length of time, number of times, posture and direction.

6. Points for attention

In addition to the four points of "Points for attention" for the Internal View of the Viscera Exercise, attention should also be paid to the following:

(1) The two ending forms as mentioned above can not be practiced one after another or mixed one with the other at one time.

(2) While doing the "self-stimulation" exercise, you may put the right and left palms towards one and the same point or two different points respectively to do the pushing, drawing, opening and closing movements.

(3) The following are the experiences I gained after a long-time practice and I offer them here to Qigong practitioners for reference who, after doing the Internal View of the Viscera for 100 days, want to learn the External View of the Viscera Exercise.

a. If the practitioner wants to practice both of the exercises at one time, he should do the Internal View of the Viscera Exercise first and then the External View of the Viscera Exercise.

b. When the weather is fine and the temperature is moderate, it is better to do the exercise of the External View of the Viscera; otherwise, do the exercise of Internal View of the Viscera.

c. The Internal View of the Viscera Exercise has good effects in curing diseases while the External View of the Viscera exercise is good for preserving health.

7. Theory of the exercise.

The External View of the Viscera Exercise can strengthen the viscera, dredge channels and collaterals, cure diseases, and preserve health, and also can improve the functions of the brain, marrow, bones, pulse and gall. Thus it plays an active role in preventing and treating diseases, protecting and strengthening health, resisting premature senility and prolonging life, and exploitation of potential energy, which, few Qigong masters of older generations mentioned during clinical treatment. Thus the Qigong exercise and its functions became a secret; only people of high Qigong accomplishments could come to realize them by their own. This was caused by historical reasons. Now I give publicity to this Qigong and offer it to the public.

In a word, this Qigong exercise is significant for the improvement of the prophylaxis and medical treatment of the Traditional Chinese Medicine. If Qigong masters and medical workers make a research into it, they will surely get something good from it.

X. Directional Qigong Exercise for Enhancing Qigong Effects and Invigorating Energy

The Method of Purplish Red Rays Shining Out

I. The Content of the Exercise

1. The pithy formula for this exercise:

A round mirror standing up to the high heaven and down to the earth.

2. There is no requirement for the posture. Sitting, walking, standing and prone postures all will do. Relax the whole body. Be in a natural and tranquilized state. The precondition of the method is to relax yourself both mentally and physically.

3. Selection of direction:

For those who take the walking, sitting or standing posture, they are recommended to do the Qigong in the fixed direction (direction of "Red Copper Mirror") I assigned to them. Their hands may be placed at any place, but they must have their palms of hands facing the front (see Fig.60). If they take a lying posture, they must have the top of the head towards the fixed direction (the same as above) and both palms of the hands upwards (in the direction of the sky).

4. Method

Relax the whole body. Slightly close the eyes (Do it with eyes open if you take the walking posture). Imagine there is a big round mirror of red copper in the fixed direction with its front facing your palms of hands and your head. Imagine that the mirror is so big that it touches with its top the heaven and its bottom the earth. Keep the imagination in a relaxed and natural state for ten minutes.

Then, imagine the mirror giving out myriads of purplish red rays of light like those from the early morning sun. Concentrate your mind on the purplish red colour of the light.

And then imagine that the cloud-like purplish red rays fly onto your body, enter it through the top of the

Fig. 60
The Method of Purplish Red
Rays Shining Out

head and the palms, spread in it and become golden rays of light illuminating the whole body. Thus imagine it again and again until you feel completely relaxed as if in a state of "saturation."

The duration of this Qigong exercise is half an hour or an hour and then bring it to an end. You can take any ending form.

II. Explanation and Points for Attention

1. Scope for application:

This exercise is appropriate for people who have experiences of Qigong practice. It can improve Qigong efficiency and exploit potential energy, so the Qigong masters who emit Qi to cure patients' diseases can use it to supply energy for themselves. For children and young people in ordinary health the exercise can improve their intelligence. For the children with exceptional function of certain organs, no matter whether they have or have no experience of Qigong practice, it can activate their exceptional functions and various potential energy in the body.

2. Frequency and duration of the exercise:

This Qigong exercise cannot follow the principle of "the more the better." It can mobilize great energy from the nature and cosmos to supply various energy including the "Three Treasures" to the human body. Thus, if people without sufficient experience of Qigong practice do it frequently, it will cause damages like those of "excess of nutrition" to health. Particularly, the patients suffering from severe diseases should not do the Qigong. They cannot do it until they have recovered from the diseases.

Therefore, a practitioner should follow the principle: "stop before going beyond the limit." He shall have a fixed time to do the exercise according to his actual conditions and the following rules:

(1) The Qigong master, who needs the supply of Qi to make up his Qi's deficiency after clinical treatment with Qi he emitted, should do it once a day.

(2) People (including children) who need to enhance the Qigong effects and exploit potential energy should do it once three days.

(3) People who enjoy good results from this Qigong exercise should do it once one or two (or more than two) weeks.

(4) The interval between two exercises should not over 100 days. Otherwise, the practitioner should do the "Gathering Qi" method in front of the "Red Copper Mirror" at the fixed place of the "Red Copper Mirror" to

increase the Qigong message. Otherwise, he will lose the effects of "long-term-fixed-direction" he has got from the Qigong.

(5) The "golden time" for the Qigong exercise is at the time period of *Zi* (11-1 a.m.) and *Yin* (3-5 a.m.) and 8-8.30 p.m.

3. "Break through" the concept of time and space. When you do the Qigong, imagine the purplish rays of light coming gently to you in an instance, no matter how far you are from the "Purplish Mirror." If you cannot handle it, you may imagine the mirror's location and form. That will have the same effect.

4. The beginners who do other Qigong exercises to cure their diseases should not do this Qigong until they have practiced Qigong exercises for more than three months.

5. Tips for those who want to do this Qigong only for a short time. For a short-time Qigong practice you may take any posture and do it in any direction. What you should do is to read silently the pithy formula and think of the mirror in the fixed direction and the purplish rays of light illuminating the whole body. This will also be able to improve the Qigong effects, exploiting the potential energy and make up the energy of the body.

6. Without a tutor's guidance one must not do the Qigong only according to a Qigong guide-book. Here the "tutor's guidance" means that the beginner, under the guidance of the author of this book, learns the direction in which he can receive energy and message, and receives a specified program of training exercises for improving Qigong effects and exploiting energy. Only after that he may practice this Qigong. In a word, this Qigong can only be learned through the tutor's oral instructions.

PART TWO

CLINICAL PRESCRIPTIONS OF THE MEDICAL QIGONG SCHOOL

Nine Qigong Massage Recipes

I. Introduction

1. The Qigong massage recipes have been proved through practices to be effective in clinical treatment with proper application.

2. In applying the Qigong massage to medical treatment do not alter or mix it with other Qigong. Otherwise, there will be bad effects on the treatment. Do not concentrate the mind, if there is no such requirement.

3. For doing the nine Qigong exercises it is required to follow the principle: "to be relaxed and natural."

4. For these Qigong exercises there is no prescribed length of time; you may handle it according to your convenience and needs.

5. You may practice any of the nine Qigong massage recipes when you do other Qigong exercises. But they and the other Qigong exercises should not be done at the same time. Each of the recipes can be applied to clinical treatment as chief or supplementary medical means. As exercises, they can be done independently or accompanied by other Qigong. As medical means they can be used together with medicines.

II. Method

1. The recipe for relieving uneasiness of mind: Stand with the body relaxed, facing a wall. Tap the wall with both palms of hands (Figs. 61 and 62).

2. The recipe for curing dizziness (including that caused by Qigong exercises) and lethargy: Press properly the two *Xiyan* (knee Eyes) acupoints with the middle fingers of both hands (Figs. 63 and 64).

3. The recipe for curing back-ache: Concentrate the mind on the Laogong acupoint (No. 8) and imagine the Qi going into the Weizhong acupoint (No. 15). At the same time tap the Weizhong with both palms of hands (Figs. 65 and 66) or send the Qi to the Weizhong with palms facing instead of touching them (Fig. 67). Assume a sitting or standing posture.

4. The recipe for improving intelligence: Do the Qigong outdoors. Stand before a tree with abundant leaves. The tree trunk should not be thicker in diameter than the arm of the practitioner. If there is no suitable trees, he (or she) may also stand before a pot of flowers in full blossom at the height of the Shanzhong acupoint (No. 3). In the latter case, the Qigong can be done indoors or outdoors.

Relax the body and stand about a meter away from the tree, facing it. Imagine gently that you are "grasping" the Qi from the tree. The imagination is accompanied by the movements of hands, grasping the Qi alternatively with one hand stretched out and the other drawn back. The movements should be slow. Look straight forward at the tree-trunk or the flowers at the eye level. Look but see nothing (Figs. 68 to 71).

The movement of hands should be accompanied by that of the tongue, which is a key part of this Qigong exercise. When stretching out the hand, drop the tongue with tongue-tip touching the lower palate; when drawing back the hand, raise the tongue with its tip touching the upper palate. The movements of hands and the tongue should be harmonized. The tongue should be relaxed. Swallow the saliva and imagine it going down into Dantian. (As to the location of Dantian, for a beginner it is a cubic area one *cun* and three *fen* inside the navel and three *cun* beneath the navel, but it is a little different from person to person. So, in practice one can decide it by himself.)

Through repeated practice of the Qigong year after year, it is proved that the prescription can improve intelligence and strengthen the brain. Therefore it is good for the mental workers of general health, patients of slight neurasthenia, and for children and young people.

5. The recipe for improving eyesight:

(1) Put the hands at half a *chi* in front of the navel with palms facing each other. Do the "open-and-close" the hands movement. When you do the "open" movement, the hands shall not over two *chi* apart from each other. When you do the "close" movement, the hands shall not touch each other. Do a quarter of an hour's "open-and-close" movement (Figs. 72 and 73).

(2) Rub the hands till they become warm (Fig. 74). Cover the eyes with the hands (Fig. 75) and put the Laogong acupoint (No. 8) directly on the eye-ball (or imagine you have the Laogong pointing to the eye-ball). When you cover the eyes, you should open the eyes and the palms should not touch them. Cover the eyes for about one minute, and then rub the hands and cover the eyes again. Each time do the exercise about ten times. The exercise can be done in the morning and in the evening, twice a day. It is advisable to do it among trees and flowers, or by the waterside.

This recipe has certain efficacy for various chronic eye-diseases.

6. The recipe for improving the poor functions of stomach and intestines:

The pithy formula is as follows: Point the Laogong to the Zusanli; slightly vibrate and send the Qi.

Method: Press the Laogong points of the hands (No. 8) on the Zusanli points of the legs (No. 9). In winter you may press the Laogong indirectly on Zusanli with trouser-legs between them; but generally, press the Laogong directly on the Zusanli, and slightly vibrate (Fig. 76).

After vibrating, have both Laogong points sending the Qi to both Zusanli points in a distance, and concentrate the mind on "sending the Qi" (Fig. 77).

The recipe can make up the deficiency of the essence, so it can cure the stomach and intestines diseases caused by deficiency of spleen and stomach.

7. The recipe for regulating the liver and gall:

Close the eyes and stand in a relaxed and tranquilized state. Slightly imagine that the liver and gall give out the Qi like black smoke, which go through the thighs and the big toes of feet and is finally expelled from the body. (Do not pay attention to the concrete route the Qi goes downwards.) Do 15 times of the imagination (Fig. 5).

Then open the eyes and remain standing (or sitting) in a relaxed and tranquilized state. Slightly press the finger on the Zhangmen (No. 5), Qimen (No. 4), and Zhongwan (No. 6) acupoints alternatively to find out the focus of disease and ache-points. The force of pressing and the duration of time should be proper and just right (Figs. 78 and 79).

Put the Laogong acupoint (No. 8) exactly above the ache-point or the focus of disease, about half a *chi* or a *chi* apart. At the same time do not concentrate the mind on it. Conclude the exercise after you feel pain at the focus of disease. The exercise should be done many times and then it can regulate the Qi mechanism of the liver and gall (Fig. 80).

The recipe is good for the liver and gall diseases caused by the blocked mechanism of the liver and gall, and it has very good efficacy on chronic ache at the liver and gall.

8. The recipe for bringing down high blood-pressure and relieving uneasiness of mind:

Any posture will do. The fingers and palms of two hands grasp, knead and press each other in all parts. Use proper force (Figs. 81 and 82). After doing the exercise for several days, you may feel pain at some points on the hands. These points should be kneaded and pressed. When old ache-points are replaced by new ones, the latter should also be kneaded and pressed until they disappear completely. Then the two hands once again grasp, knead and press each other with even and proper force. Generally, when the exercise produces such effects, it will have palliated the disease or cured it completely.

However, if there are no such ache-points, the exercise will also produce good results. The lack of ache-points are due to two reasons: the first one is that different people may have different effects; the second one is that efforts made on it are not sufficient. Therefore, more efforts should be put in doing the exercise. It is proved through practice that the key point of attaining good results is not decided by whether there are the ache-points or not but by how hard you practice the exercise.

The recipe is good for apoplexy caused by high blood-pressure, and coronary heart disease.

9. The recipe for raising the Pure Qi and dredging the channels:

Cross the fingers of both hands as if making a bow with hands folded in front and put them in front of the Tiantu acupoint (No. 2, Fig. 83). Imagine that you have a feeling of taking a bath with warm water, which flows gently upwards from the waist to the head (covering the whole back) and then downwards from the head and face to the chest and abdomen. Pay no attention to what route it flows along, nor think of blood vessels and channels. Put the mind on the bath as if there is warm water flowing all over your body. While doing the Qigong, you are recommended to slightly close the eyes. But, if you feel better with eyes open, do not close them.

The recipe is good for "chronic apoplexy" caused by low blood-pressure and low blood-sugar as a result of descent of Qi in Zhongjiao (the middle heart).

Fig. 61 Recipe for relieving uneasiness of mind.

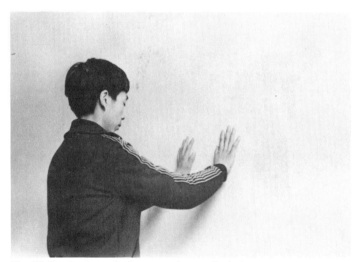

Fig. 62 Recipe for relieving uneasiness of mind.

Fig. 63

Recipe for during dizziness and lethargy.

Fig. 64

Recipe for during dizziness and lethargy.

Fig. 65

Recipe for curing back-ache.

Fig. 66

Recipe for curing back-ache.

Fig. 67
Recipe for curing back-ache.

Fig. 68 Recipe for improving intelligence.

Fig. 69 Recipe for improving intelligence.

Fig. 70 Recipe for improving intelligence.

Fig. 71 Recipe for improving intelligence.

Fig. 72

Recipe for improving eyesight.

Fig. 73

Recipe for improving eyesight.

Fig. 74
Recipe for improving eyesight.

Fig. 75
Recipe for improving eyesight.

Fig. 76
Recipe for improving the poor functions of stomach and intestines.

Fig. 77
Recipe for improving the poor functions of stomach and intestines.

Fig. 78

Recipe for regulating the liver
and gall.

Fig. 79

Recipe for regulating the liver
and gall.

Fig. 80

Recipe for regulating the liver
and gall.

Fig. 81

Recipe for bringing down high
blood-pressure and nourishing
the mind.

Fig. 82

Recipe for bringing down high
blood-pressure and nourishing
the mind.

Fig. 83

Recipe for raising the Pure Qi
and dredging the channels.

PART THREE

TEN METHODS OF MEDICAL SCHOOL QIGONG FOR MAINTAINING HEALTH

1. Ward off sickness by walking.

The method is one of the treasured Qigong methods of Medical School. It is appropriate for patients with chronic diseases and puzzling diseases who, however, can walk in an ordinary way. It is also a good exercise for people in good health or with Qigong experiences to maintain health or improve Qigong effect. Its main part is fast walking supplemented by tranquilized sitting. The method can cure many chronic diseases.

"Walking as fast as the wind" is the key point of the Qigong. It means to walk fast with strong and vigorous strides. But at what speed and how far one should walk would be in accordance with his physical ability. The desired Qigong effects of the walking is that after walking one is full of vigour, feel completely relaxed mentally and physically, and the symptoms of disease disappear or become fewer. (At the beginning the practitioner may feel a little tired and have a slight ache at the waist and legs, but it is a normal phenomenon.) Otherwise, you should readjust the walking in order to attain best results.

"Sitting as stable as a bell" is the necessary course to be taken before and after the walking. It means you should sit as stable as a bell. You may think but should not be confused in mind. You may take any posture but your body should be as upright as the string of a musical instrument. When sitting, imagine there is a golden ring of light around the navel. Slightly put the mind on the ring. It is proper to sit for a quarter of an hour (1-2 minutes will also do).

A saying has it that "It is reasonable to combine activity with tranquillity." The combination of "walking as fast as the wind" and "sitting as stable as a bell" will make "warding off sickness by walking" possible.

The modern scientific research also proves that walking fast can improve the functions of heart system and respiratory organs, lower the quantity of cholesterol in blood an prevent high blood-pressure. In a survey conducted by Japanese scientists in a village known for a great number of old people enjoying long-life it is found out that the people there all have the habit of walking fast.

Walk one or two times every day, each time about half an hour. Walk at an even, steady and rhythmic pace. Walk in a relaxed state. After the walking improves your mental and physical health, you may walk longer and faster. If you keep on doing the exercise, you will surely benefit from it.

2. Eat radish in winter and ginger in summer

It is very hot in summer and cold-dampness is gathered inside the body. In the hottest days of summer people tend to suffer from dysentery and the stomach is often affected by cold pathogen. So, in order to get rid of cold pathogen and dampness, people should eat ginger in summer.

In winter it is very cold and the heat is gathered inside the body. People tend to suffer from the symptoms of disease such as inflammation of nasal and oral cavities, cough owing to the heat of lungs, constipation, etc. The stomach is often affected by the heat. So, in winter people should eat radish to relieve the retention of food in the stomach and to regain the transporting and digestive functions of the spleen and the stomach, and to clear off the heat and eliminate toxin.

As to how to eat radish and ginger, there is not special rules for it. You can eat it according to your habit.

3. Fast for 24 hours to treat the cold

In order to treat a cold, fast for 24 hours (or 36 or 48 hours if the cold is severe). When you feel hungry during the time, you may drink water. (Water can desalinize hydrochloric acid in gastric juice, overcome the hunger, purify the body and help to cure the disease.) But you should not drink too much at a time, nor drink nutritive beverage, so as not to have bad influence on the dietetic treatment.

However, the hunger therapy cannot be applied to the following people:

(1) patients suffering from shock caused by low blood-pressure, low blood-sugar and insufficient supply of blood to the brain;

(2) patients of severe diseases;

(3) people above 80 years of age; and

(4) people weighing less than 30 kg.

Correct application of the method can shorten the duration of the cold without the help of medicine. It has been proved that the hunger therapy is effective for an intractable cold.

4. Foot-washing therapy for promoting health and preventing diseases.

Prescription: ginger (sliced) 100 grams,
　　　　　　　Chinese pepper 100 grams,
　　　　　　　green tea 50 grams, and
　　　　　　　rice vinegar 250 grams.

Put them in half a basin of water and have them boiled. Put the feet in the steam of the boiled water and when the water becomes not so hot, put the whole feet into it. Do it once every evening. A dose of the medicine can be applied for 3-7 days. If you insist on doing this for a month, you will find that the foot-washing therapy can warm the lower limbs, strengthen the waist and kidney, improve the functions of ears and eyes, and develop intelligence.

5. Six pithy formulae can bring out good health.

The Qigong of Medical School has six pithy formulae, which can bring out good health. The six pithy formulae are as follows:

> Don't speak too much,
> Don't think too much,
> Don't eat too much, and
> Don't drink wine too much.
> Suppress your anger as soon as possible and
> Moderate your sexual life.

They are very useful for maintaining good health. According to the traditional Chinese medicine, speaking too much would injure the Qi, so speak only what is necessary; thinking too much would injure spleen, so one should think reasonably in an orderly way and clear the mind of impure thoughts; eating and drinking too much would injure stomach and intestines, so one should take food and drink properly. Excessive smoking and drinking would bring endless troubles; anger would injure liver; sexual desire is something necessary to a human being, but it should not be excessively stimulated. One should put attention to these six pithy formulae and to put them into practice. This is the best way of prolonging one's life and preventing diseases and maintaining good health.

6. Restoring the hearing of a deaf-person.

Put 50 grams of jasmine tea and 50 grams of Chinese pepper into a new thermos bottle and then cork the bottle. When you need to use it, uncork it. Let the deaf person put his or her ear at the mouth of the bottle and imagine that he or she can "hear" the "sound" in the bottle. As to how long and how many times the patient should do the exercise, it should be decided by the patient himself or herself.

The method can be applied to sudden deafness and

inductive deafness caused by Yin deficiency of liver and kidney, but not to the deafness caused by organic diseases.

Attention: don't put water into the bottle. Plug in the cork after each treatment. The tea and Chinese pepper powder should be replaced in six months.

7. Strengthening the kidneys and enhancing the Qi for the male.

Pithy formula: Close your mouth when you move the bowels and pass urine, and you will live a long life.

Method:

(1) When you pass urine, close the mouth, clench properly the teeth, inhale but not exhale (exhale if you need to), and lift the heels up. Having passed urine, draw up the anus for one minute, then restore ordinary breathing and end the clenching of teeth.

(2) When you move the bowels, close the mouth, have the tongue touch the upper palate, clench properly the teeth, and do not speak.

Kidneys are the postnatal essence. The method can enhance the Qi, strengthen the kidneys, and consolidate teeth and marrow. A man will get good results from it, if he makes a habit of carrying out the pithy formula.

8. Method for improving female's health method:

(1) Tap both sides of the chest for 3-5 minutes.

(2) Close the eyes and put the mind on the part underneath the tongue. When the saliva increases, send it with mindwill to both feet. (The whole course takes not more than ten minutes.)

The method is good for the female's diseases such as liver stasis and blocked channels. Don't practice the first part of the method during pregnancy period. If a woman persists in doing this exercise, it can cure her diseases, strengthen her health, improve her looks, harmonize the Qi and blood, and invigorate her energy.

9. Method of improving the looks

The method is good for improving the looks and eliminate skin-freckles. The effects of the Qigong can be seen in a month.

(1) Tap the top of the head and neck with finger-tips of both hands for 2-3 minutes.

(2) Massage the face with both palms upwards from the lower chin to the forehead for 2-3 minutes. (Do not do it downwards.)

(3) Massage the face from both cheeks to the neck (downwards) for 2-3 minutes.

(4) After doing the above exercises, apply a proper amount of your favorable fruit juice to the face.

Do the exercise once a day (in the morning or in the evening).

10. Clasp both hands to strengthen the heart and improve intelligence

The method is good for neurasthenia, insomnia, amnesia, and heart disease. Besides, it can relieve one of brain fatigue.

Method:

Clasp both hands (as if you are applauding). The louder the better. (Clasp in a clever way. Do not hurt the palms.) At first, 10 minutes will be enough, and then the time for the exercise can be prolonged properly.

There is no limitation on the number of times for the exercise.

The method is very simple, but its theory is profound. Since the fingers link up with the heart, the clasping hands can dredge the three Yin and three Yang channels and collaterals and thus cure the heart and channel diseases. As a result, intelligence will be improved. The effect of the Qigong can be seen in a month.

PART FOUR

DRILLS OF THE TREASURED QIGONG OF MEDICAL SCHOOL

I. Introduction.

The drills of the Qigong of Medical School are wonderful exercises for improving Qigong effect and exploiting potential energy, and also a powerful measure for performers to improve Qigong cultivation and drive the "sleepy demon" away.

Performers, no matter whether they have attained the essentials of Qigong basic training or not, what physical conditions they have, and from what Qigong school they have learned, male or female, old or young, strong or weak—all can get good results from the drills.

It has been proved that the drills can improve the Qigong effect, exploit the potential energy, cure diseases and maintain health, strengthen the body and mind, and improve intelligence and prolong life. The drills are very simple and easy to learn, but the theory is profound. They will not cause deviation. The performers will get twice the result with half the effort.

The drills, taking advantage of the excellent environment at midnight, overcome sleepiness. It is a clever way of carrying out the drills. Thus the drills can enhance to the maximum the performer's "three treasures," i.e. the essence of life, Qi and spirit, and achieve the greatest successes.

II. Three Basic Drills.

Drill 1

Assume a sitting posture from 23.50 to 00.10 at midnight (with crossed legs or simple sitting posture). Face the direction where there is a scenic spot with picturesque scenery. (It doesn't matter whether you have visited it or not, or how far it is. But you should know its location, distance and characteristics.) Slightly concentrate your mind on it. Imagine that you look at it and hear it. "Scan" it in your mind. Slightly close the eyes and be relaxed mentally and physically. After 20 minutes, conclude the exercise.

Points for attention:

1. Each time have only one target for scanning instead of two or more targets.

2. You may use one and the same place for your target for several times successively, or only once and change to another place the next time.

3. Do not be pleased at or afraid of what appears physically or mentally during the exercise.

Drill 2

During the period of the day from 11 p.m. to 1 a.m. (*Zi-shi*) be seated on a soft cushion on the ground or a bed, facing the south, with eight glass cups full of water, which are placed evenly around the cushion, two *chi* away from the body, in eight directions (four in the east, south, west, and north respectively, and the other four in four corners). The cups in the south and north should be due south and due north, so they should be placed by means of a compass.

Close the eyes and be relaxed mentally and physically. After half an hour exhale turbid Qi eight times (prolonging the exhalation naturally). At the same time conduct turbid Qi away from the seat of disease (such as the six internal organs) by means of imagination and expel it through the mouth out of the body. But inhale through the nose without imagination. Inhale and exhale eight times and then open the eyes. Drink the water in the cup at the back (in the north) and through imagination conduct the water to the Dantian point below the navel.

Then close the eyes and be seated in a tranquilized state for half an hour. Do the above breathing exercise eight times and drink the water in the northeast. Repeat the breathing exercise until drink up the eight cups of water clockwise. The whole exercise takes about four hours.

Points for attention:

1. Drink the water in the exact order (north, northeast, east, southeast, south, southwest, west, and northwest).

2. Breathe naturally. Do not do it with force.

3. Those who do not drink cold water may fill the cup to the half in advance and pour hot water into it before drinking.

4. Don't force yourself to drink too much. Drink only a proper amount of water.

Drill 3

In the hour period of *Zi* (11 p.m.-1 a.m.) put a big candle at the right center of a washbasin and pour water into it until the basin is half full. The practitioner may stand or be seated, facing the candle (there is no limitation on the distance), with the eyes half-open, in a relaxed and tranquilized state. Place both hands about half a *chi* away from the navel. Make a hand-movement of kneading a ball softly and imagine that the "Qi of water and fire" from the basin moves continually into the "ball" held in the hands. There is no time limitation on the duration for the exercise. Before ending the exercise, draw both hands with the imagined "ball" close to the navel and imagine that the ball moves into the navel. Then cover the navel with hands, one hand on the other. Sit or stand in repose with hands on the navel. Do not focus the mind on anything. After 15 through 30 minutes end the exercise.

Points for attention:

1. As to the duration of the hand-movement of kneading the imagined ball, the practitioner can handle it properly.

The time for covering the navel should not be less than

15 minutes.

2. The practitioner may shift their posture at any time when sitting or standing.

III. Six Special Drills

Time for the drills: from 23.00 hours every night.

1. The Drill for Promoting the Qigong Effects and Activating Potential Energy.

Put 50 grams of Chinese prickly ash, ginger and green tea respectively in half basin of water, and have the water boiled. Put the feet over the water and let the foot-arch be steamed in it. Then put the feet in the water when it becomes not so hot. At the same time be seated, close the eyes and relax the whole body. Raise the right hand and the left hand up over the head alternatively with the index finger pointing to the sky and then draw them down to the chest. Repeat the hand exercise until the water becomes cold. Get the feet dry and end the drill. The medicated water for the drilling can be used for five times, but before each time it should be boiled. After five days it should be replaced by fresh water.

2. The Drill for Keeping a Cool Head and Refreshing Oneself.

Sit up straight, facing north. Cover the navel with both hands (You may put the hands over the clothes). Close the eyes and relax the body. Slightly focus the mind on the Big Dipper. Do the drill for 20 minutes.

3. The Drill for Keeping Sharp Eyes and Promoting Intelligence.

Put 100 grams of jasmine tea in a small cloth bag and seal the bag. Sit up in a tranquilized state, relax the body and close the eyes. Slightly tap the head and forehead (Don't tap the eyes!) with the tea bag. Imagine that you are holding a ball of fire and its flames move into the head. Do the drill for 30 minutes and end it.

4. The Drill for Eliminating Pathogens.

Close the eyes and sit up. Relax the whole body. Face a pot of flower, any flower will do except cactus, or a pot of green plant without flowers, about a meter away from the body. Focus the mind on it for about 10 minutes and then open the eyes. Grasp the seat of disease with hands over the clothes. Imagine that you have grasped the disease Qi, and throw it onto the flowers. Notice that you hands should not touch any part of your body or your clothes. Grasp only in the air. Practice 30 minutes and then end it.

5. The Drill for Promoting Memory.

Sit up, facing north. Close the eyes and relax the whole body. Stretch the hands out about half a *chi* away from the navel, with one palm of hand upwards and the other downwards and fingers pointing to the north. Imagine that fire emits out of the palms of both hands. After 10 minutes turn the palm of the upward hand downwards and the other upwards.

Keep on the same imagination for 10 minutes. Raise up both hands with palms slightly swaying over the head, about half *chi* away from it. Practice 10 minutes or more and then end the drill.

6. The Drill for Overcoming Sleepiness.

Sit up and close the eyes. Face any direction. Slightly inhale three times. Imagine you are exhaling turbid Qi through the mouth. Cover the navel with both hands (or over the clothes). When you are sleepy, softly tap the top and back of the head as well as the neck with finger-tips (be sure to tap softly). When you are no longer sleepy, cover the navel with both hands again. Thus repeat the exercise. The drill will take at least one hour. It can strengthen the essence Qi of the "Three Treasures," promote memory and keep an orderly mind, and thus overcome dozing over a book and being absent-minded at class.

PART FIVE

SOME EXAMPLES SHOWING THE EFFICACY OF THE QIGONG OF THE MEDICAL SCHOOL

1. The following are some of the cases of the Qigong practitioners who have benefited from Qigong practices. The materials were written by the Qigong practitioners themselves. There are many such cases, but owing to the limited space of the book, we can select only a small part of them for reference.

2. The cases are based on original materials written by the learners themselves. However, the materials were revised owing to the following reasons:

(1) The praising words which do not concern the Qigong exercises are deleted.

(2) The materials are of great length and thus the unnecessary parts are deleted.

3. Through practice it has been proved that the Qigong of Medical School has great curative effects and there are many people who have benefited from it. How-

ever. it does not mean that the Qigong can cure all diseases. As the Chinese Medicine and the Western Medicine each has its own strong points and weak points, the same thing is true with the Qigong of Medical School. Besides, it should be noted that the Qigong takes the internal training and self-cultivation as its main part and takes the external force from outside as its supplementary part. Therefore, in order to get good results from doing Qigong, it is necessary to have a strong confidence in it, but this does not mean to worship it blindly. If we all hold an objective and scientific attitude towards Qigong, such an attitude surely will give a spur to the flourishing development of Qigong.

(A) Case Studies

Case 1
Patient's Name: Wang Guangxin
Sex: Female
Age: 37
Occupation: Teacher at the Chaoyang Normal School, Beijing

I have suffered from Beheet's syndrome for eight years. Last year I was so ill that I was confined in bed. Afterwards I began to learn to practice the Qigong of Medical School under the guidance of Master Huang. One year's Qigong practice has produced a marvelous effect on me.

Beheet's syndrome is a refractory disease, for which there is no cure in the world. It can be controlled only with hormone, but the curative effect is not good. So the disease pains the patients deeply. In 1982, unfortunately, I contracted this disease. I suffered from low fever and sleeplessness. It seemed as if there was a fire burning in my heart. There were ulcers at several parts of mucous membrane, which gave me much pain. I went to some big hospitals to obtain medical attention. My disease was diagnosed as Beheet's syndrome. Doctors said, the disease was due to inferior ability of immunity. The difficulty to cure it is only second to that to cure cancer. With medical treatment by a doctor at Dongzhimen Hospital my disease was controlled by and large.

However, in the early 1989, I suddenly had low fever and sometimes high fever. I was always so tired that I could not take a step, and I felt so thirty that I could not stop drinking water. My saliva was sweet. I thought I had diabetes. But chemical examination showed it was not. I became thinner and thinner. In June I had a relapse of Beheet's syndrome. After a month I suffered so much from the disease that my looks became haggard. My friends and my family went around to look for folk prescriptions for me. But no prescription worked.

Fortunately, a friend of mine introduced me to Qigong master Huang Runtian. Master Huang began to give Qigong medical treatment to me. It brought about immediate good results. At that time I had low fever and was very weak. I lost my hair whenever I combed it. Mucosa ulcer confined me to bed for five months and I suffered from great pain.

Master Huang came to cure my disease. At the first treatment he made a pail of Qigong water and asked me to put my feet in the water after it was boiled. I did it for seven days and learned Qigong exercises of the Medical School under his guidance. As a result, the symptoms of the disease lessened. On the seventh day the ulcer healed up. So I could go downstairs to do the exercises. I got rid of the disease finally. I felt as if I was given a new life. I did not know how to express my thanks to Master Huang, who did not take any pay for the treatment from me, and even did not drink a cup of water in my house when he came to cure my disease. Whenever I think of it, I am deeply moved and feel uneasy about it.

When he came to my house for a second time, he made another pail of Qigong water and asked me to drink a cup of it every day. After drinking the water I felt the heat in my body was eliminated gradually and felt comfortable and relieved. Then Master Huang and his students came twice to cure my disease by emitting Qi together, which had very good results. I felt the Qi coming into my body, which made me feel a tingle and heat. Then, for a week in a row, I felt very cold all over as if I had fallen into an ice cavern. But at midnight I felt so hot that I could not bear having a quilt on my body. Since then all the symptoms of low fever, heavy legs, cracked skin on hands, rheumatism have disappeared.

Three months later, the spring came and I, like a dry tree given a new life in spring time, was full of vitality again. I gave up all medicine and medical treatment gradually, but persisted in practicing the Qigong under the guidance of Master Huang conscientiously. Every day I did it for seven or eight hours. I did "The Qigong of Invigorating the Kidney and Adjusting Qi" and "Postnatal Development Qigong" three times a day and "The Unification of Mindwill and Qi Exercise" at the hour period of *Zhi* (11 p.m.-1 a.m.). When I did the Qigong exercises, I concentrated my mind on them and was in a cheerful state of mind. For doing the "The Qigong of Invigorating the Kidney and Adjusting Qi" I sat for a quarter of an hour and patted the underside of the arch of the foot 900 times. Each time after doing it, I felt the Qi and blood in my body were regulated and I was full of vigour, just as the *Wen-Yang-Yu-Zheng-Jing* Canon states: "The wonderful result is the great happiness in the body. Other people will find your looks are improved a lot."

After doing the Qigong for half a year, thirty or forty red spots appeared at the underside of the foot arch and disappeared a week later. After practicing it for a year the Yongquan acupoint seemed opened. I often felt there was a pain at the underside of foot arch and the pathogenic Qi was removed through the point. Thus I have a firm belief in the Qigong and preserved in doing it. As a result, the balance of Yin and Yang in my body was recovered and I was full of vigour. Now I can climb Mt. Miaofengshan (1,290 meters above sea level) and Mt. Jiulongshan and walk tens of miles without a break. It seems as if I am physically quite another person than what I was.

The Qigong of the Medical School is also very efficacious to insomnia. Last year I suffered a lot from insomnia owing to my disease. I could not fall asleep even after taking five sleeping pills, but after doing the "Qigong of Invigorating the Kidney and Adjusting Qi" (*Tong-yuan-ji-ji-gong*) for the first time I fell asleep without taking a sleeping pill. Insomnia was a chronic and stubborn disease from which I suffered a lot. However, after doing the "Qigong of Invigorating the Kidney and Adjusting Qi", especially the "Drill for Overcoming Sleepiness," my sleep was much improved. In the past I could not fall asleep if I went to bed after 10 p.m. But now when I go to bed at 2 a.m. after doing the Qigong exercise "Overcoming Sleepiness," I can sleep so well that I do not have a dream and at the daytime I am full of vigour and do not need to have a nap after lunch. So I advised all my friends who also suffered from insomnia to do the Treasured Qigong of the Medical School, and they all achieved good results.

A year's Qigong practice has conferred an inestimable benefit upon me. Now I still continue to do the Qigong exercise to consolidate and develop the Qigong's good effects on me. The Qigong of the Medical School has simple method and remarkable effects in improving health and exploiting potential Qi.

Written on February 20, 1991

Case 2
Patients' Names: Wang Yuzhen and Liu Haiqing
Address: Room No. 2, 89 Qinghua Road,
        Baishi Village, Yantai City

My name is Wang Yuzhen, female, 53. I am a retired worker. I have suffered from backache for 24 years. Last year when I was told that Qigong Master Huang came to give a curative treatment on Nanhong Street, I went there for the Qigong clinical treatment. As there was such a big crowd of people around the master in the house, I had to sit by the side of the street to take the treatment as the master ordered. The Qigong treatment, for only one time, much relieved me from the 20-year-long backache. From October last year till now I have been in a cheerful state of mood, I am very happy because I become healthier.

So, when Master Huang come to Yantai this time, my husband Liu Haiqing and I also came to Yantai to obtain another treatment. As a result of a three-day-treatment, the pain in my legs disappeared, and my husband was relieved from sciatica. We felt as if we were younger by more than ten years. We are much grateful to Master Huang, who can bring the dying back by a miraculous cure.

Case 3
Patient's Name: Wang Wenxin,
Sex: Male
Age: 60
Address: Dahedongcun Village, Wanggezhuang Town,
        Muping County, Shandong Province
Time: May 20, 1989
I suffered from arthritis at both legs, and high blood pressure. After attending Master Huang's Qigong treatment, my diseases were cured a lot. Then I took Master Huang's another treatment for two days. After that I was recovered from the diseases. I could stretch my legs without feeling any pain; my blood pressure returned to 140/90 mmHg and it has never risen again. During the 17 days from the treatment till now, I never feel tired before midnight when I do the Qigong exercise instead of sleeping. I am fully convinced of Master Huang's Qigong medical treatment. It is my great honour to be treated by him and to learn the Qigong from him. I shall do all the exercises Master Huang asked me to do.

[We made a follow-up visit on Wang Wenxin in June 1990, and found that his diseases had been completely cured by Qigong and that he had become a strong supporter of Qigong in the locality.]

Case 4
(The following is a letter from Zhang Rongying to Qigong Master Huang.)
72 Qiaoxi Tiejunshan, Jining City, Inner Mongolia.
Dear Master Huang:
I benefited very much from your Qigong treatment. On the first day when you gave Qigong lessons to us, I was suffering from spasm of the stomach and I had not slept or taken food or water for a whole day. Your miraculous Qigong relieved me from the pain. I felt as if

there were warm water flowing in my body. I was relieved from suffering. On the next day I took another treatment from you. After that my heart disease and kidney disease were much cured. What was more wonderful was that the extra liquid in my body mostly disappeared, I lost weight by more than ten *jin*. Now I can move about quickly. I feel as if I had become a quite different person. In a word, I am very happy and excited. It is your miraculous Qigong which saved. The incident is the happiest event that I cannot forget. Master Huang, I will be grateful to you all my life. I wish your Qigong message will stay in my body forever and I will always be as warm as in the springtime.

Best wishes

Sincerely yours,   Zhang Rongying

[Note: The case happened at the National Qigong Clinical Application Training Class sponsored by the Jiuxianqiao Qigong Training Center affiliated to the Beijing Qigong Research Association in the middle of March 1988 at the assembly hall of the General Station of Diplomatic Correspondence at Shiliju to the south of Jiuxianqiao.]

Case 5

(A brief summary made by Hao Qinghui, female, 64, a pediatrician-in-charge on March 20, 1989. Her address: 36 Dafangjia Hutong, East District, Beijing.)

I learned a lot at the Qigong Training Class in the past few days. As to how much I have learned I cannot express it in language, because, to a person who learns Qigong conscientiously, to learn it is an important event in his life and Qigong will be passed down from generation to generation, how can he estimate how much he has learned?

At the class I learned Qigong theory and practice from Master Huang. What is more important is that I learned a lot from his moral character and devotion to the cause of Qigong.

The way and effects of his Qigong medical treatment

are miraculous. At the class when he gave treatment by the way of remote control, I made an observation of two patients by means of *Shuang-mang* (double-blindness) method, who suffered from chronic gastritis and chronic bronchitis respectively. The treatment had immediate good results. Till now the treatment was not known to the patients, who do not learn Qigong and do not believe in it.

Besides, last year when Master Huang gave Qigong medical treatment by way of remote control at a class in Shanghai, I also gave the treatment to two child-patients who were in Beijing and Shanghai respectively. The child-patient in Shanghai suffered from infection owing to BCG vaccination, and the one in Beijing from upper respiratory tract infection. With Master Huang's Qigong treatment these two children were soon recovered from the diseases. The infection owing to BCG vaccination is difficult to cure with medicine. Generally, for a child the upper respiratory tract infection is a minor disease and does not need Qigong treatment. As a pediatrician, I know quite well that for a child the symptoms of low fever and cough will last several days, no matter what medicine is taken. However, with Master Huang's Qigong treatment, the Beijing child's symptoms of low fever and cough disappeared in half a day. What a miraculous event it was!

The above mentioned four patients were not given any psychological suggestion, because till now they did not know they were treated by means of Qigong. That was the miraculous result of Master Huang's Qigong treatment.

I attended the training class for the purpose of learning from Master Huang the method of improving health and curing diseases. I did not intend to cure my disease. However, in those days of attending the class I had ease of mind and was full of vitality. I used to sleep 7-8 hours a day. But after attending the Qigong class I slept only 4 hours and did not need a nap after lunch. In the nine days I took only a nap. Besides, I no longer suffered from the pain owing to insufficient supply of blood to the heart, and since the 11th day of this month I have not taken any medicine.

Written on March 20, 1989

Case 6

I am 62 years old. I have been deaf for 40 years. I could not hear unless other people spoke loudly to my ears. Yesterday I could not hear what you (Master Huang) said at the opening ceremony of the Training Class, but after the first curative treatment I was able to hear. I feel very happy.

Written by Zhang Changshan for Fu Jin'er
October 11, 1988

Fu's address: 9-15 Yukai Street, Yantai City
[This case happened at the Training Class of the Treasured Qigong of the Medical School held in Yantai in October 1988.]

Case 7

[The following is a letter written to Master Huang by a patient named Wang Shufeng. He is a staff member of the Planning and Dispatching Section of Passenger Service of Shandong Yantai Motor Transport Company.]

October 13, 1988

Since 1984 I have suffered from rheumatic arthritis and facial paralysis. I suffered also with insomnia and timitus. In February 1985 I went to Beijing to take medical treatment at the Capital Hospital. An examination showed there was a small tumor at my tonsil. So I had to submit to a surgical operation in the hospital. After the operation, I felt stiff in the tongue and could not speak well. Besides, my mouth itched. My face also itched whenever it touched cold water. It made me feel unwell. I went about to visit doctors. I was told it was a chronic disease that could not be fully cured. I suffered a lot economically and mentally. Even in the hot summer days I had to wear heavily. However, as a result of the treatment I recovered a little from the facial paralysis. But it left behind sequelae: my mouth was wry and I could not see clearly. Looking at my wry mouth I felt sad with tears in my eyes.

When I was told that you, Master Huang, was coming to hold a Qigong training class in Yantai, I felt very happy. But it was a pity that the class would be held only in six afternoons. I wondered if you could do the treatment in such a short time. When I attended the class I found there was a special atmosphere. Master Huang, you have a deserved reputation. After the first day's treatment at the class I had headache and toothache, I thought perhaps it was because the Qi had affected on the focus of disease as you had told us. On the second day I no longer had the pain and was full of vigour. At the class, when you emitted Qi, I felt the Qi surrounded my body. Tears gushed from my eyes suddenly, and I felt as if a power was drawing my mouth from the right side to the left for 5 or 6 minutes. I was very happy. I told my companions by my side what I felt. Thus my wry mouth and strabismus, which caused me much pain, were cured by the Qi treatment. I felt happy and relaxed. After the treatment I went home and found I could go fast downstairs carrying a barrel of rubbish. However, the Qigong treatment did not have good effects on the ringing in my ears. But I believe it will be cured if I persist in practicing the Qigong as you, Master Huang, instructed.

With my best wishes,

Sincerely yours,   Wang Shufeng

Case 8

[Ding Lansheng, associate physician-in-charge with the clinic of Beijing Western District Housing Administration, wrote to the author on March 10, 1988 as follows:]

When I attended your Qigong training class yesterday, there was a fragrant smell, similar to that of sandalwood. At the class, my feet grew numb with Qi.

In recent days the effects were as follows:

1. I no longer had the pain caused by scapulohumeral periarthritis and I could move my arms freely.

2. I felt comfortable and relaxed, and was light at

steps.

    3. I slept for fewer hours but still was energetic.

    Besides, I gave a long-distance Qigong treatment to my husband for his chronic angina and hoarse voice. At that time he caught a cold. He was very busy with his work. With the treatment he was cured a little of the angina.

    Finally, I would like to express my sincere gratitude to you and Beijing Western District Baijia Qigong Association. I will go on with Qigong practice and will try to relieve patients of their pain as you do.

Case 9—On the marvelous efficacy of the Treasured Qigong of the Medical School.

    [Liu Jixin, a female patient, 49, manager of Yantai Zhendong Store, wrote a letter to the author on 14 February 1989 as follows. Her address: 29-3 Baichun St., Yantai.]

    At the previous Qigong training class you cured me of cholelithiasis. (It can be proved by the results of B-supersonic examination of my body.) I could not forget it. On this class you cured me of cervical vertebra disease.

    This afternoon when you emitted Qi outside the house, I felt that my neck stiffened and my head was hot as if it was roasted on the fire. Half an hour later my head was no longer hot. But I had a pain on the neck. The pain moved from one joint to another. When it moved to the fifth and sixth joints, I suddenly felt relaxed at both shoulders. When I turned my neck, it did not sound like two pieces of wood rubbing as it did before. Instead, I felt relaxed at the neck, shoulders and legs. The neck disease, which I had suffered from for such a long time, was cured at last. I am very happy. Here I would like to show my sincere thanks to you, Master Huang.

Case 10

    I am now 54 years old, male, working in a college. On October 10, 1988, I attended the Qigong training class held by Beijing Qigong Master Huang Runtian in Yantai. Under the inducement of the *Pigu* (fast) message given by Master Huang, I entered into the *Pigu* state for ten days, from October 12 to 22. In the first five days I drank only a little water. In the second five days I took only a little thin millet gruel and fruit. Till early November I ate only a little gruel, salted vegetable and fruit.

In those days I was full of vitality. The Qi in my body moved smoothly. I had a merry heart and very good state of mind. I read and wrote with good results.

[The original article was published in the journal *Dongfang Qigong* (Oriental Qigong), p.32, vol. 3, 1989. The author of this article was Sun Weiyuan, working with the Department of Physics of the Yantai College of Education.]

Case 11

My name is Liu Aiying. I am 27 years old. I live in Shunzhengxin Village in Muping County, Shandong Province. I am grateful to Master Huang because he cured not only me but also my son of our diseases. I suffered with allergic bronchial asthma and I had to take a lot of medicine when I was in pregnancy. Thus my child can not walk now even when he is three years old. I have been always worried about him. Medical treatment did not work with him. Yesterday at the class Master Huang emitted Qi to give a long-distance treatment to my son. When I went home after the class, I found that my son could walk by himself for about twenty steps. It was a miraculous event. I was very happy. My mother was also very happy.

My mother said: "Yesterday at about 4 o'clock in the afternoon, the child suddenly refused to be carried in my arms and tried to walk by himself. I do not know why." I told her it was the power of Master Huang's Qigong.

[It happened at the training class of the Treasured Qigong of the Medical School held in Muping County, Shandong Province in May, 1989.]

Case 12

[Patient: Tang Xiaoming, female, 42, a teacher with the Yantai Middle School of Overseas Chinese.]

In the summer of 1979, a student shot accidentally at

my right arm with an air gun and a surgical operation was made to take out the bullet, but my nerve in the arm was injured during the operation. After that my right arm became powerless and I could not clench my right fist. After Master Huang emitted Qi on my right arm, it became energetic and I could clench the fist again.

Besides, with the treatment, I was recovered from the symptoms of feeling depressed at the chest and gasping for breath caused by coronary disease.

I am grateful to Master Huang and the Qigong Association for it inaugurated the Qigong training class. I will persist in doing Master Huang's Qigong to improve my health for the cause of education.

Written on February 16, 1989

Case 13

[Patient: Wang Xuemin, male, 53, a worker in the Factory of Lock of Muping County, Shandong Province.]

I suffered with leucopenia (white blood cells reducing) owing to chronic benzene poisoning. Since April 1984 when the disease was diagnosed, I had been hospitalized in the Yantai Hospital of Occupational Diseases for three years. Injection and medicine did not work. I had 3,000-3,500, not more than 4,000 white blood cells and my haemochrome was only 7-8 grams.

From the second half of last year to April this year, all four tests showed that I had only 7 grams of haemochrome and I suffered with anemia. Because of some reasons I could not continue to be hospitalized though doctors asked me to. Instead I had to take medicine at home.

On May 18, 1989 I attended the Qigong training class held by Master Huang. The class lasted only three days. In order to find out whether the Qigong treatment was effective I went to have a blood test after work on May 20. The test showed that the white blood cells rose to 6,900 and haemochrome was 9.41 g. This is close to normal index. It is miraculous, though it can not show that my disease is completely cured. Now when I go upstairs to the fourth floor, I will not lose my breath and be difficult to take a step as I did before.

I am grateful to Master Huang and will do what he asked me to do in order to have my disease completely cured.

Written on May 20, 1989

(Attached to this document is an original blood test report made by the People's Hospital of Muping County, which proves what the patient said was true.)

Case 14

[Patient: Yang Leyan, female, 30, who worked in the Yantai Boiler Factory.]

This is my first report on the results I got from the Qigong training class. I think, you, Master Huang, will also be pleased to know it.

I suffered with a tumor, 2.6 X 2.3cm. in my left ovary. On the first day of the Qigong training class, I had a severe pain at my abdomen. As I had experienced it before, I could not be sure whether it was due to the influence of Qigong or not. On the third day at 7 o'clock in the evening blood flew out of my vagina. I began to understand it was the influence of Qigong.

This morning I went to the People's Hospital and had a B-supersonic test made for me. The test showed the tumor had disappeared.

I do not know how to show my thanks to you, Master Huang. I hope you will come to Yantai again.

Written on January 16, 1989

Case 15

Patient: Zhu Rulan, female, 53, a staff member of the Editorial Department of Serbian Language of China International Broadcast Station.

The patient suffered with high blood pressure and heart disease for more than 30 years. In several tests of her heart the electrocardiogram showed her heart was in abnormal state. At the end of 1990 an electrocardiogram made in the People's Hospital affiliated to Beijing Medical University showed: T-wave changed. HBD showed: cardiac arrhythmia, poor heart-synchronism and insufficient supply of blood by cardiac muscle. She suffered from the symptoms of dizziness, depression in the chest, palpitation and asthma.

On November 26, 1990, she attended the training class of the Treasured Qigong of Medical School held in the Naval General Hospital. She began to practice the *Tong-yuan-ji-ji-gong* (The Qigong of Invigorating the Kidney and Adjusting Qi). On December 1, she felt much better and the above symptoms became not so serious as before. On December 5, another electrocardiogram was made for her in the hospital, which showed that her heart was in a normal state.

Case 16

[Patient: Qu Ying, female, 36, works at the Boiler House of the Beijing Labor Bureau. Address: 2 Huaiboshu St., Xuanwu District, Beijing.]

Last September I attended the Qigong training class held by Master Huang Runtian. Since then I learned the Qigong and benefited from it. Before that I had suffered with neurasthenia, mastitis, and stomach disease. I always took medicine and easily felt tired and fretful. After attending the Qigong training class, I got unexpected good results from it. The above-mentioned diseases disappeared miraculously from my body. I found myself in a pleasant and relaxed state which I had never experienced before.

The Qigong of the Medical School has absorbed all the strong points of other Qigong schools. Its exquisite theories, concise exercises and miraculous efficacy hold a special attraction for numerous Qigong fans. The Qigong of the Medical School has many originalities. The "Drill for Overcoming Sleepiness" is one of them. "Not to sleep day and night" seems unrealistic to ordinary people, but if you use Qigong to replace sleep, you will fully realize that it is possible.

I think "overcoming sleepiness" is a direct challenge to the traditional concept. It breaks the old routine, brings the human potentiality into full play, and make it fully conform to the regular pattern of nature. Therefore it is a matter of great significance.

At first, I did not have a clear understanding of "overcoming sleepiness," but I attended an "overcoming sleepiness" course five days in a row just to have a try at it. I got unexpected success. Those who took part in the practice were old men, middle-age people and young people. There were mental laborers and physical laborers of all occupations. During the process of "overcoming sleepiness" they all persisted in their normal daily life. Experiences proved that "overcoming sleepiness" is a test of the endurance of the human body. Human being have enormous potentialities. To break through a limitation will lead to a leap. Human ability, such as the ability to adapt oneself to circumstances, resistance to diseases, the ability to suffer hunger and thirst, the ability to stand intense heat and coldness, and the ability to endure fatigue, etc. will be much stronger in the Qigong state than in non-Qigong state.

I think, the so-call "overcoming sleepiness" does not means not to sleep a wink. When a person is doing Qigong exercise, sometimes he is in a light sleep and this gives him a high-quality rest and banish his fatigue. Sometimes to sit in a quiescent state for two or three hours is very good for relieving fatigue and restoring energy.

Since I learned to do the Qigong of the Medical School, the time for my sleep greatly reduced, but I feel very energetic and never feel tired. I believe if I persist in doing the Qigong, I surely may make a break-through and completely overcome the desire of sleep.

Written on 7 March 1990.

(B) Statistics of Qigong Efficacy

1. Certificate on the Efficacy of Qigong of the Medical School

Time: September 10, 1989.
Place: 1 Sanlihe Zhong Street, Western District, Beijing.

Sponsor: China Qigong Science Research Society.
Attendance: 500.
Duration of the class: 2 weeks.
Lecturer: Huang Runtian.
1. The number of patients who after attending the first class got remarkable results and recovered their health: 141
2. The number of attendants who performed various exceptional function of certain organs after the Qi stimulation: 214
3. The number of those who, after attending the class, were stimulated to fast: 23
4. The number of those who had remarkable effects on enhancing Qigong effects and invigorating energy: 176
5. The number of those who reduced time of sleep to a half while their energy greatly enhanced: 156.
6. The number of those who smelled fragrance during exercises: 313
7. The number of those who did not do the Qigong as instructed: 329
8. The number of those on whom the Qigong had no effect: 102.
9. 59 children learned the Qigong for Increasing Intelligence; 32 of them through stimulation achieved instant efficiency.

The Teaching Group of the Qigong
Theory and Method Committee
of the China Qigong Science Research
Society (Seal affixed)

2. Certificate on the Efficacy of the Training Class of Qigong of Medical School

At the invitation of Weifang Chemical Fiber Factory, Beijing Qigong Master Huang Runtian organized a Training Class of Treasured Qigong of Medical School in Weifang from 12 through 17 of May, 1986. The class was given 7-10 p.m. every day, during which time Master Huang emitted Qi to cure the sick and enhance the attendants' Qigong effects and invigorate their energy, and gave lectures on the Qigong's theory and methods. Most attendants benefited from the class. The following is the statistics of efficacy collected from the class:

1. Completely cured: 99.
2. Fundamentally cured or improved: 451.
3. Cured by long-distance emitted-Qi: 233.
4. The number of attendants who performed various exceptional function of certain organs after the Qi stimulation: 251.
5. The number of those who, after attending the class, were stimulated to fast: 41.
6. Those whose wrist-watches were disturbed when they were having the drill of concentrating the mind-will: 33.
7. Those who smelled fragrance during doing exercises: 388.
8. The number of those on whom the Qigong had no effect: 15.

Weifang Chemical Fiber Factory
(Seal affixed)
May 17, 1989

3. Summary of the Training Class of the Qigong of Medical School

The Qigong Science Association of the Ministry of Commerce organized a Qigong Training Class of the Medical School in the auditorium of the Nuclear Ministry from July 17 through July 22. Master Huang Runtian was invited to give lectures and teach the Qigong, altogether 12 class hours. About 160 people attended the Training Class; most of them had contracted diseases of various kinds to a certain degree. After six days' learning the statistics of efficacy is as follows:

1. Completely cured: 23.
2. Fundamentally cured: 118.
3. Those who had marked progress in enhancing the Qigong effects and invigorating energy: 60.
4. Those who smelled fragrance when doing exercises: 87.

5. Master Huang emitted Qi for the benefit of a part of attendants' relatives who were not at the class and got good effects: 49
6. Cured patients by means of message objects and got effect:49
7. Those whose wrist-watches were disturbed when they were having the drill of concentrating the mind-will: 12.
8. The number of those who, after attending the class, were stimulated to fast: 33.
9. The number of those on whom the Qigong had no effect: 7.

Secretariat of the Qigong Science Association
of the Ministry of Commerce (Seal affixed)
July 31, 1989

4. Certificate of Statistics of the Efficacy of the Training Class of the Treasured Qigong of the Medical School

At the invitation of the Qigong Science Research Society of the Muping County, and the Senior-Cadre Bureau of the Muping County, Beijing Qigong Master Huang Runtian came to Muping County to open a training class of the Treasured Qigong of the Medical School for six days, from May 18 to 23 1989. A total of 1659 people attended the class. Master Huang emitted Qi to cure the attendants, to enhance their Qigong effects and invigorate their energy, and gave lectures on the Qigong's theory and methods. Statistics show that

1. The number of those whose diseases were completely cured: 213
2. Those whose diseases were fundamentally cured or improved: 1443
3. Master Huang emitted Qi for the benefit of a part of attendants' relatives who were not at the class and got good effects: 47
4. Master Huang cured patients by means of message objects and got effects: 418
5. The number of attendants who performed various exceptional function of certain organs after the Qi

stimulation: 564.
6. The number of those who, after attending the class, were stimulated to fast: 44.
7. Those whose wrist-watches were disturbed when they were having the drill of concentrating the mind-will: 74.
8. Those who smelled fragrance when doing exercises: 1278.
9. The number of those on whom the Qigong had no effect: 69.

We hereby certify that the Qigong of the Medical School has profound effect, is welcomed by the attendants and has made a sensation in Muping.

Muping County Qigong Science
Research Society (Seal affixed)
Senior-Cadre Bureau of the Muping
County Party Committee (Seal affixed)
May 23, 1989

5. Training Course of the Qigong of Medical School

Sponsor: Labour Union of the Beijing Glass Instrument-making Factory
Lecturer: Huang Runtian
Time: 6.30-8.30 p.m., from July 24 to July 29, 1989.
Health condition of the attendants: Over 90% have various chronic diseases.
The number of attendants: 165.
Place: The Meeting Room, fourth floor, Glass Instrument-making Factory.
Statistics on Efficacy

1. The number of those whose diseases were completely cured: 22 people, making up 13.3%
2. Those whose diseases were fundamentally cured or improved: 138 people, making up 83.6%
3. The number of those whose diseases were cured or improved by means of taking food containing Qigong-message: 643 people, making up 38.8%
4. Master Huang emitted Qi for the benefit of a part of attendants' relatives who were not at the class and got

remarkable results: 31 people, making up 18%
5. Those who had marked progress in enhancing the Qigong effects and invigorating energy: 111 people, making up 67.3%
6. The number of those who, after attending the class, were stimulated to fast: 36 people, making up 21.8%
7. Those who smelled fragrance when doing exercises: 109 people, making up 66.1%
8. Those whose wrist-watches were disturbed when they were having the drill of concentrating the mindwill: 29 people, making up 17.6%
9. The number of those on whom the Qigong had no effect: 3 people, making up 1.8%
10. Total efficacy: 98.2%

Labour Union of the Beijing
Glass Instrument-making Factory
(Seal affixed)
July 31, 1989

6. Statistics of Efficacy of the Training Class of the Treasured Qigong of Medical School

Time: From November 26 to December 1.
Place: The Qigong Immunization Clinic of the Naval General
Hospital, 6 Fucheng Road, Haidian District, Beijing.
Lecturer: Huang Runtian
Attendants: 96
Statistics of Efficacy
1. The number of those whose diseases were completely cured: 22
2. Those whose diseases were fundamentally cured or improved: 67
3. Those who emitted Qi for the benefit of relatives at another place by means of emitting Qi and got remarkable results: 12
4. Cured patients by means of message objects and got effects: 40
5. Those who had marked progress in enhancing the Qigong effects and invigorating energy: 65

6. The number of those who, after attending the class, were stimulated to fast: 35
7. The number of those whose appetite became stronger: 26
8. The number of those whose sleep was reduced to half the amount it used to be, while their energy was improved: 70
9. Master Huang taught children to learn the Qigong for Increasing Intelligence and Activating Body Energy; 15 of them achieved instant efficiency.
10. Those who smelled fragrance when doing exercises: 54
11. The number of those on whom the Qigong had no effect: 1

The Qigong exercises taught in this Training Class are as follows: "The Qigong of Invigorating the Kidney and Adjusting Qi" (*Tong-yuan-ji-ji-gong*),

"The Qigong of an Internal View of the Five Parenchymatous Viscera" (*Wu-zang-nei-jing-gong*),

"The Basic Qigong Exercises for Universal Illumination and Emitting-Qi" (*Pu-zhao-bu-qi-gong*), etc.

We should further exploit the Treasured Qigong of the Medical School and bring it into full play for the benefit of the people.

The Application Committee of
China Qigong Science Research Society
(Seal affixed)
December 2, 1990

Graphic Representation of Some Important Acupoints

Number	Acupoint Name	Position
1	Yintang	The middle point in the linking line between the two eyebrows
2	Tiantu	Right in the center of the suprasternal fossa
3	Shanzhong	On the anterior median line, horizontal to the two nipples
4	Qimen	Right below the nipple, between the sixth and the seventh rib
5	Zhangmen	On the eleventh costal end
6	Zhongwan	4 *cun* above the navel
7	Dantian	The area 1.3 *cun* inside the navel and 3 *cun* under the navel
8	Laogong	In the palmar center, between the second and third metacarpal bones
9	Zusanli	Approximately 2 cm outside peribial crest
10	Yinbai	On the inside of the big toe, 2.1 *cun* from the corner of the nail
11	Yongquan	At the center of the sole, in the fossa formed when the toes and metatarsus are bent
12	Baihui	Right at the top of the head, at the fossa in the center
13	Shenshu	1.5 *cun* sideward from below the spinal process of the fourth lumbar vertebra
14	Mingmen	Below the spinal process of the second lumbar vertebra
15	Weizhong	At the center of the cross striation of the pepliteal fossa
16	Huiyin	Between the two *yins* (the anus and the genitalia)

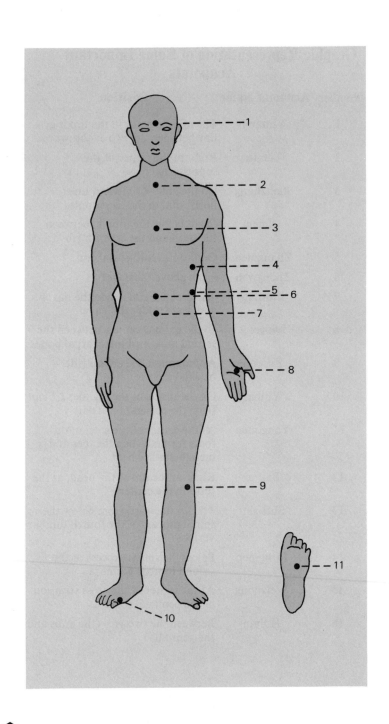

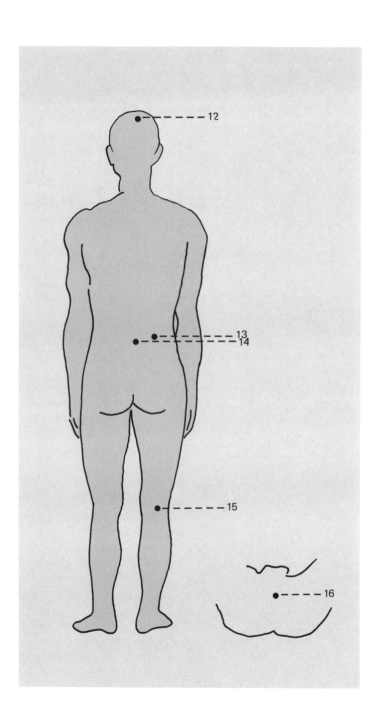